Resurrecting Easter

Meditations for the Great 50 Days

Kate Moorehead

Morehouse Publishing
NEW YORK · HARRISBURG · DENVER

Unless otherwise noted, the scripture quotations
contained herein are from the New Revised
Standard Version Bible, copyright © 1989 by the
Division of Christian Education of the National
Council of Churches of Christ in the U.S.A. Used
by permission. All rights reserved.

Morehouse Publishing
4775 Linglestown Road
Harrisburg, PA 17112

Morehouse Publishing
19 East 34th Street
New York, NY 10016

Morehouse Publishing is an imprint of Church
Publishing Incorporated.
www.churchpublishing.org

Cover design by Laurie Klein Westhafer
Typeset by Denise Hoff
Library of Congress Cataloging-in-Publication Data

Moorehead, Kate, 1970-
   Resurrecting Easter : meditations for the great 50 days /
Kate Moorehead.
      pages cm
   ISBN 978-0-8192-2848-2 (pbk.) -- ISBN 978-0-8192-
2849-9 (ebook) 1. Eastertide--Meditations. I. Title.
   BV55.M58 2013
   242'.36--dc23

                              2013023004

Printed in the United States of America

Contents

Introduction

He was an eccentric ninety-year-old man who loved to sunbathe in his backyard. He was also one of the most brilliant biologists who ever lived, winner of the Kyoto prize in biology and a professor at Yale. His name was Evelyn Hutchinson.

Every Sunday, without fail, Professor Hutchinson would drag his old, decrepit body down the aisle at church to receive holy communion. His back was bent from osteoporosis, but he managed to get down on his knees at that rail and hold out his hands for the mystery of the bread and wine.

I was a student at Yale at the time, and Professor Hutchinson heard that I was going to seminary. After church one Sunday, he asked me a question.

"Are you going to preach about the Word of God?"

I nodded, wondering where he was going with this.

He craned his neck to straighten himself up enough to look me directly in the eye.

"I'll tell you, Kate," he said. "If I had to preach, do you know what I would do? I think I would have to stand up in the pulpit and do this . . ."

Professor Hutchinson raised his shriveled arms to the sky, and shrugged.

For centuries, churches all over the world have observed the season of Lent. Immediately after his baptism, Jesus walked out into the desert for forty days and fasted and prayed. So we too fast, pray, and take on some special discipline during Lent. And then, when the forty days are over, we celebrate the resurrection and have a big party on Easter.

But there is a significant problem with this practice. You see, the early Christians did not believe that Easter was just one day. Easter was an entire season of feasting, a season that lasted for fifty days. It was supposed to trump Lent in length and intensity. We were supposed to celebrate the resurrection for that long.

But today, we observe Lent. We do our disciplines. Then we celebrate Easter on a Sunday. We hunt for chocolate eggs and dress up. The music is great and lots of people flood the church. But by Monday morning, life goes back to normal.

Why don't we observe the Great Fifty Days? I don't think it's because we don't like parties, or we refuse to celebrate. I think we can't celebrate for that long because we have forgotten how to sustain joy. We simply don't know how.

Jesus did not appear just once after he died. He appeared over and over again, in different ways, over a period of forty days. On the fortieth day, his body was physically lifted up into heaven in front of the disciples. And on the fiftieth day, Jesus gave us the gift of the Holy Spirit to inspire us so that we could continue to do God's work in the world.

The whole thing is so mind-boggling, so otherworldly, that it does make me want to climb up in the pulpit and just shrug my shoulders. Resurrection is the heart and soul of Christianity. It is the reason we exist, the reason why a peasant who walked and taught along the shore of Gallilee for three years and died on a cross might still be remembered today. Because he came back to us. He lives still.

The early Christians called the event of the resurrection the Mysterium Tremendum. The great mystery. It cannot be rationalized or broken down into sound bytes. Our minds will never understand what happened. Even the greatest thinkers like Professor Hutchinson know that it is too much for our small brains to master. It can only be glimpsed through the stories that the disciples and others told about how Jesus returned and what he said to them.

This book is an invitation to celebrate the resurrection. This is a series of fifty meditations, focusing on the appearances that Jesus made to specific disciples, to Mary Magdalene, to Peter, James, Paul, and Thomas. We will glimpse the visions of the book of Revelation and the gift that Jesus gave us in the Holy Spirit.

There are many different theological understandings of resurrection. Does it occur immediately at the moment of our death, or do we wait for the end of days? Is the physical body raised or just a spiritual body? Paul, John of Patmos, and others do not seem to agree on all these questions. I do not believe that these questions can be adequately answered in this life. All that we can do is stick very close to the words of scripture and, through those words, try to see a bit more clearly.

Resurrection is not something that can be grasped by the rational mind, not in its entirety. But it can be glimpsed through the stories that we have been given. Come with me and let us look at how Jesus Christ rose from the dead.

The Resurrection and the Sabbath

And on the seventh day, God rested from all that He had done. (Genesis 2:2)

It is amazing to me to think that God rested. The Almighty, the maker of the universe, rested. It means that rest comes from God. It does not originate in human beings. Rest is holy. It is sacred. It is the stuff of God.

After Jesus' death on the cross, he could have risen immediately. After all, he was God's son. Surely he had the choice to rise immediately. Certainly, he could have popped back up and reappeared on the Sabbath. But instead, he chose to rest. He chose to postpone the most incredible miracle of all time in order to be still. That is how important, how holy it is to rest. The resurrection itself waited on the day of rest.

In some Christian traditions, it is taught that Jesus descended to the dead and spent three days rescuing souls. This makes it sound like he was very busy during that time, but I prefer to think of him as resting. Do I believe that the resurrection redeemed those who had already died but who loved God? Absolutely, I do. But I think that linear time does not always pertain to God and we can certainly believe that this was accomplished at some point. After all, what is a day in the mind of God?

It is vital to remember that the time of rest came even in

the midst of the single greatest act of God. God will not be rushed. Even resurrection waits.

How much does this impact the way that we as Americans run our lives? If Jesus rested and waited to rise from the dead, even as the disciples cried and grieved, then shouldn't we rest, even in the midst of events that we think are life-changing?

Life is enhanced through the process of reflection, waiting and resting. It is not laziness to make time for rest, it is wisdom. Rest allows us a period in which to absorb the beauty and magnificence of life. True rest makes us more fully alive, more like God.

Week 1

....

Mary

DAY 1 The Truth

Returning from the tomb, they told all this to the eleven and to all the rest. Now it was Mary Magdalene, Joanna, Mary the mother of James, and the other women with them who told this to the apostles. (Luke 24:9–10)

In order to experience the miracle of resurrection, you must first face the fact that you are going to die. Mary Magdalene saw the risen Christ at the tomb. She had to go there, to that dark place where death lay visible for her to examine. It was in the face of death that she found life.

Most Americans run away from death. We euphemistically say that someone "passed away." We talk about our 401Ks as if we are preparing to live in retirement forever, but we do not prepare for death.

Most of us seem to believe that if we avoid the subject of death, maybe death won't happen to us. Maybe if we use Oil of Olay and work out enough, and watch our cholesterol, then death won't come for us.

When people in their eighties get cancer, many of them are shocked. They ask, "Why did God do this to me?" as if God has tricked them out of their lives. One woman, at eighty-nine, asked me as she lay on her deathbed why God was punishing her.

"Why is God doing this to me?" she said.

I tried to talk to her about the inevitability of death, that all bodies grow old and die, but she did not seem to hear me. "My dear friend," I said, "didn't you know that the death rate is 100 percent? Our bodies were simply not designed by God to last forever. They run out of juice. Your body is old and worn-out. It is time to talk about dying."

This is the best part of my job as a priest. I get to tell the truth. I get to come into people's homes and ask if they have thought about dying, if they love God, if they say their prayers, if they are ready. Often my bluntness shocks them. Many will cry. Many will tell me that they really want to go, but their loved ones will not let them. One woman begged me not to let her husband put her on life-support when the time came for her to die.

Our hospitals are designed to fight death with everything we have. Doctors are made to feel like failures if they do not "save" a life. But what often ends up happening is that they end up prolonging dying, not saving life. I cannot count the times when I have begged families and doctors to allow patients to die. People get so confused. They actually think that it is a sin to let a loved one who is terminally ill and on life-support die. But they are only prolonging pain and suffering. Part of life is letting go and there is such a large difference between love and attachment.

You cannot contemplate resurrection without looking at the tomb, without contemplating death. There is no other way to eternal life but through death itself, through the tomb. We don't just continue life as we know it. Life doesn't just go on uninterrupted. We must die first and only then can we hope to live in Christ.

If you admit that you are going to die, then your life can become a love letter to God. You can think of your life as a gift, the gift of a limited period of time in which you can choose how to serve God. And you can prepare for your death so that it is beautiful and edifies all those who love you.

How can we understand the miracle of the resurrection if we do not look into the tomb and see the darkness? Death is coming for you. It will come. And the only thing that you will be able to cling to is your belief in a God who loved you enough to face death for you.

Being Yourself with God

Early on the first day of the week, when it was still dark, Mary Magdalene came to the tomb and saw that the stone had been removed from the tomb. (John 20:1)

When I was a child, Molly Smith was my best friend. A simple chain-link fence with a small gate connected our backyards. We went through that gate a lot. She would come over to my house. I would drift over to hers. We skateboarded in the neighborhood and vowed to never wear dresses. I cannot imagine my childhood without Molly.

Molly was no good at sports. She never could get her feet to move fast enough. She seemed to be perpetually falling down. I would laugh at her, pressure her, tell her to move faster. I thought that she was lazy.

Molly and I collected stickers. We loved our sticker albums with a passion. I had more stickers than Molly and I loved rubbing it in.

After we graduated from high school, Molly and I went to separate colleges. In the spring of my sophomore year, I got a call from my mom. Molly's roommate had found her in a coma. They'd rushed her to the hospital, where the doctors discovered that she had too much fluid on her brain. It had been building up for her entire life. That was why she was clumsy and bad at sports. If her roommate had not found her, she might have died in her dorm room.

I felt terrible for all those years of laughing at her and

yelling at her to run faster. I never knew why she couldn't respond with more energy.

I found my sticker album and made Molly a large card. On it, I tried to fit every single sticker I owned.

Mary Magdalene had something wrong with her brain. In biblical times, when someone was sick in a way that no one could see or understand, they diagnosed the problem as demons. Epilepsy, schizophrenia, mental illness of any kind, when people hurt themselves or others for no visible reason, their afflictions were attributed to demons. If there was no other visible cause for an abnormality, pain, or suffering, it was called a demon. And Mary had seven demons. Seven different kinds of pain and suffering. Seven things that no one could explain.

So Mary suffered. She was not herself. She lived in a world of misunderstanding and pain.

Then Jesus came and when he came, everything changed.

Jesus did not punish Mary for her demons or lecture her. He healed her. And for the first time in her life, she was truly herself.

Once Mary discovered herself in Jesus, she would not leave his side. She could not bear to be away from him. He was everything to her. Mary Magdalene alone was present at the foot of the cross in all four of the Gospel accounts. She never left Jesus, even when he was bleeding and dying. Not even the horror of the cross could drive her away.

On the third day, when the sun began to rise, she raced to the tomb. She must have felt like half of her heart was removed when he died. She was drawn to his body almost unconsciously, needing to be there with him, even in death.

Mary's first response to the disappearance of his body

was shock and grief. She wept. Maybe she could not see through her tears. Maybe she just could not conceive of him being alive, but when Jesus appeared, she did not recognize him.

Jesus called her back to herself. It is so fascinating to me that he didn't identify himself. He didn't say, "Hey, it's me! Jesus!" Instead, he said *her* name. He named her.

"Mary."

He brought her back to herself, as he had when he healed her. And she woke up to the resurrection life, to the fact that he was there all along, that he lived, and that she lived in him.

I have always been afraid that I might simply blend into some kind of divine morass in heaven, that it might be somewhat like a drop of water hitting the ocean, my soul simply swallowed up by God. Though this might sound good to some, it sounds scary to me. But this story of Mary's encounter with the risen Christ tells us something important. Mary recognized the resurrected Christ when he knew her, when he spoke her name. She recognized resurrection because the resurrected Christ knew her. Could it be, then, that we will be known in heaven by the risen Christ, that he will call our names as well?

DAY 3 To Those Who Loved Him . . .

But Mary stood weeping outside the tomb. (John 20:11)

Mary Magdalene loved Jesus. When he died, her heart was broken.

It is vital to begin contemplation of the resurrection by realizing that Jesus appeared to those who loved him. Jesus did not appear to Pilate or Judas. Jesus did not appear to the high priest, the centurion, or the Pharisees. In the Gospel accounts Jesus appeared only to his disciples and friends.

Most of these disciples had failed him completely. Peter abandoned him and denied even knowing him. The majority of his disciples fled his crucifixion, leaving him to die a violent death without their presence or support. But despite all their failures, these people did love Jesus. It was that love that kept their relationship with him intact, even when they abandoned him to die.

Jesus appears first to the women. The women did not abandon Jesus at his death. The women were the first to appear at the tomb. Hence they were first to see evidence of the risen Christ. In all four of the Gospels, Mary Magdalene alone is present both at the cross and at the tomb. No wonder she was the first to see the resurrected Christ.

What does God mean to tell us by revealing the risen Lord only to those who loved him? I believe that the message is simple.

You cannot taste eternal life if you do not love God.

It is love, not intelligence, not good behavior, not even the highest kinds of morality that draws the soul to God. All good behavior is a fruit of the love that must exist between the believer and God.

Jesus' great commandment is true. If we want to live beyond this life, then our way forward is clear. Jesus spelled it out for us when he said, "Love the Lord your God with all your heart, and with all your soul, and with all your mind. . . . And love your neighbor as yourself" (Matthew 22:37–39).

It makes me wonder what would have happened if no one had loved Jesus. We would have missed out on the resurrection.

God did not reveal the risen one to those who did things perfectly, to those who said the right things or never made a mistake. God revealed the risen one to those who loved him, who longed for him.

DAY 4 Marriage in Heaven

Jesus said, "For when they rise from the dead,
they neither marry nor are given in marriage, but
are like angels in heaven." (Mark 12:25)

We do not hear of Mary Magdalene again after the resurrection accounts. Unlike the other disciples, we have no record of Mary going out into the world to preach the gospel. Her preaching was finished when she told the disciples that Jesus was alive. We do not hear about Mary Magdalene in the book of Acts or in the epistles of Paul. Her first and last words are recorded on that first day of the week when she proclaimed, "I have seen the Lord!" From that point onward, she is silent. How strange that one of the most important women in all of scripture seems to just disappear.

The love that Mary felt for Jesus was so strong that it jumps off the pages of the Gospel. More than any other disciple, she could not leave Jesus. She adored him. Mary's adoration of Jesus has caused scholars and novelists alike to surmise that Mary and Jesus were married or at least that they were having sex. After all, when Jesus appears at the tomb, he tells her not to hold him, the implication being that she was planning on putting her arms around him. Did they have a physical relationship?

In the middle of his earthly ministry, Jesus tells the disciples that there will be no marriage in heaven. No one will be given in marriage and there will be no issue if a woman dies who has had many husbands. In other words, in the resurrection life there is no longer sex, or marriage, or any kind of coupling.

People will often ask me if they will see their loved ones in heaven. I believe that they will but the love we feel here for our family and friends and even for our spouses is a small part of the greater love that exists in God. All love will become clear to us as coming from God in heaven.

Mary did adore Jesus. But I believe that her love was far above and beyond sexual love. It was a love that released her from her demonic possession and caused her to serve him all the days of his life. It was a love so complete that she could not leave him when he hung on the cross, or after he died. And after he rose and ascended into heaven, she was simply quiet. Perhaps Mary's heart was full; perhaps she had nothing more to say.

Day 5 Attachment

Jesus said, "Don't hold on to me." (John 20:17)

When Jesus appeared to Mary Magdalene in the resurrected form, she wanted to hold on to him. He had to tell her not to hold him, for he had not yet ascended to God. Jesus belonged to God. He could be loved, but he could not be held.

In my years as a priest, I have learned that there is an enormous difference between love and attachment.

Anna was a woman who had waited to get married. She wanted to find the perfect man. By thirty-eight, she began to realize that the perfect man might not be out there, so she settled for a good man. And once they got married, they immediately began to try to have children.

Anna had wanted to be a mother her whole life. Her happily-ever-after consisted of a husband and two kids, a boy and a girl. When she gave birth to first a girl and then a boy, she thought that life had reached its peak. She was beginning her happily-ever-after. And she loved her children. Oh, she loved them. She stayed at home to take care of them, focusing on every detail of their lives, from their diet to their clothing to all their activities. She was the perfect mom.

But her children began to have behavioral issues fairly early on. Her daughter seemed angry and would throw dramatic temper tantrums. Her son seemed unfocused, dazed. And the more her children did not behave, the harder Anna tried. She was consumed with anxiety. Her children had everything children could ask for, so why were they not behaving? She gave them *everything.* She loved them so much. Yet they were angry.

"I love my children," she would say. "I give them everything that they need: food, shelter, clothing. Why are they not behaving? Why are they not happy? What is wrong with me?"

Anna loved her children, but she was also attached to them. She no longer saw them as unique individuals. She was constantly comparing them to what she wanted them to be. It was their job to fulfill her expectations and when they didn't, she became more controlling and they became more angry. She really couldn't see them at all, not as God made them.

What Anna failed to do was to let go of her expectations. She never simply asked herself, "Who are my children? What are they trying to tell me? How can I give my life to them?" Instead she worshipped an idol, a vision of family that does not really exist. She thought that she loved her children, but she was in love with an image of them. In her desire to make them fit her ideal, she was suffocating them.

The people we love the most are those who are paradoxically the hardest to truly love. Our love for them gets so easily coated over with expectations, attachments, guilt, and other issues. We find ourselves not listening to the ones we truly love. We want them to be the people we want them to be, not the children of God that God has created them to be. The longer that we live with others, the less that we listen to them. Our disappointment with them looms so large that it can prevent us from seeing them at all. "Fulfill my expectations," we tell them. "Do what I need and want."

And we no longer listen to the ones we supposedly love the most. We just hold onto them.

I cannot tell you how many times I have sat in hospital rooms with someone who is clearly longing to die, yet their loves ones will not let them go. I will ask the family members, "Who is this about? Is this love or is this attachment? Is this about meeting your needs, or is it about meeting the needs of the person you love? Is having your loved one around really better than letting go when you are causing undue pain and prolonging the dying process? Whose needs are being met here?"

There is no way to enter the resurrected life without letting go of this physical life. That means letting go of your stuff as well as the people to whom you are attached. You cannot bring anyone or anything with you when you die. I believe that God calls us all to practice letting go even before we die, to practice the art of loving without attachment.

DAY 6 Fixing What Is Broken

But she did not know that it was Jesus.
(John 20:14)

My grandpa was a handy man and loved the outdoors. He loved to fish, to hunt, and to build just about anything. His garage was his workshop, full of tools and wood of all kinds. He loved to make lamps out of driftwood from the sea.

When I was about five, my grandpa made me a beautiful kite of paper and hollow bamboo. We went to the beach on Sanibel Island to fly the kite. I ran as fast as my little legs would carry me and the kite rose up in the sky, higher and higher into the wind. He laughed and clapped, too old to run but happy to watch.

As I ran, I did not see a high lifeguard chair in front of me. "Watch out for the chair!" Grandpa called, but I paid no attention. I ran the kite right into the chair just as it was being launched. The kite got stuck on the rails of the chair. I pulled harder. "Careful!" Grandpa warned. I did not listen but just pulled harder. The kite snapped in two.

I watched as half the kite spiraled down to the ground. The rest of the kite remained tangled in the chair. It was a mess. I ran back to inspect the damage. It was ruined.

I was devastated. I sobbed. I could hardly put my despair into words. "IT BROKE!" was all that I could say. "IT BROKE!" Tears poured down my face. I found it hard to breathe through the sobs. My beautiful gift was wrecked and it was my fault.

Grandpa came over. He looked at the broken kite. He looked at me. His eyes were sad. He let me cry awhile. He put his hand on my shoulder.

Then he said, "I can fix this."

Jesus healed Mary Magdalene of her demons. He did that for many people. He healed people of demons more than he taught. He did it all the time. When Jesus saw people who were broken, he said, "I can fix this." And he did.

Mary was different from all the others. You see, most of the people healed by Jesus were grateful to go back to their lives or their families. But Mary had no one. Once she was healed, she wanted to be with Jesus all the time. He was her family. He was her everything. The reason that she loved him so much was because she remembered how broken she had been before he came. Her life had been a complete disaster, and she never wanted to go back to that life again.

Mary Magdalene is perhaps the most unappreciated, unrecognized, and misunderstood of all of Jesus' followers. She is not counted among the twelve disciples because she was a woman. But she was with Jesus all the time. She never left. When Jesus was captured and other disciples fled, Mary stayed. She followed when Jesus' body was taken away to be laid in the tomb of Joseph of Aramathia. And it was Mary who was the first to arrive at the tomb on the morning after the Sabbath, just as the sun was rising.

When Mary sees that the tomb is empty, she runs to get the disciples. When they too see that the body is gone, they run off. Mary breaks down. She sobs and weeps alone by the tomb. Everything in her world is over. She no longer has even Jesus' body as comfort. She has nothing. She is alone again. Everything in her world has broken apart. And then he comes.

The resurrection is so overwhelming that Mary cannot see it at first. She doesn't recognize Jesus because his presence was too good to be true. How could something so broken be fixed? It seemed impossible.

There is nothing that God cannot fix. Nothing. You may have terminal cancer or alcoholism. You may have been laid off from your job, or your marriage has crumbled. You may have treated your loved ones terribly, or someone close to you may have died, and you feel as if your life has just cracked down the middle, that nothing will ever be the same again. But God says to you, "I can fix this."

Wait for a few days. Let the sun rise. In time God will fix all of it. God will rise. You may not get what you expected. You may not get the solution you want. Like Mary, you may not even recognize God's answer when it comes. But God will rise.

DAY 7 Light Shines in the Darkness

And very early on the first day of the week, when the sun had risen, they went to the tomb. (Mark 16:2)

In 2012, the head at Episcopal School of Jacksonville was shot to death in her office by a young teacher who had been fired that morning. The young man then killed himself.

The school had been born from St. John's Cathedral in Jacksonville. As dean of the cathedral, I serve on the school's board of directors. My son was a seventh grader there at the time of the shooting. The head of school was my friend.

When I heard the news, I rushed to the campus.

The school went into lockdown, and within forty-five minutes, students were safely escorted to the cars of their parents. I prayed with the faculty as they heard the news. And the hardest days of our lives began.

The first few days after the tragedy were a blur as we rushed to console students and provide ways for them to return to campus. The headmaster's funeral was enormous and beautiful, under a great oak tree at the school. As I preached, I kept wondering why everyone was looking up into the sky. After the service, someone showed me a picture of a rainbow that had appeared. It arched right over the place where we were remembering the life of this inspirational woman. I was glad that I had not seen it during my sermon, because when I saw the picture I burst into tears.

After the chaos of the week of the murder, spring break

came. Then classes were due to resume. Life had to return to some kind of normal routine. And that's when things got even harder.

Part of me wanted to pretend it hadn't happened, but there was this empty space where my friend had been. The office where she had died was an empty hole. Nothing seemed the same.

Mary Magdalene and the other women saw the first signs of resurrection when they went straight to the truth, to the dark hole that was left in their lives when Jesus died. It was there, in the emptiness that they realized something had happened. If they had not gone back to that dark place, would they have missed his rising?

If someone is grieving, it is good to talk to them about their loved one who has died. Some people think it may cause more pain to do this, but I believe it is helpful to go directly to the source of their pain rather than trying to avoid it. After all, everything reminds them of what they have lost. They have not forgotten the one they love, even for an instant. Talk about it. Go there with them, to their pain and their suffering. Let them take you there.

Week 2

....

Peter

Jumping In

When Simon Peter heard that it was the Lord,
he put on some clothes, for he was naked, and
jumped into the sea. (John 21:7)

My eight-year-old was daring me to jump into the pool. "Come on, Mom! You can do it!" It was a rather cold February day in northern Florida, and I'm a wimp about cold. But Max and I had been gardening and he wanted to play. He is constantly trying to get me to stop working and play with him. It's his way of trying to get me to live into the resurrection life.

I whined. I balked. And then I jumped.

It was freezing! I hated how it felt. I got out immediately, soaked to the core. Max was laughing. And I realized that I had just had the best moment of my day. I was proud of myself for jumping into the water.

Peter sees the risen Lord, and he can't wait. He jumps into the water and does everything he can to hurl his body toward the Lord. He no longer makes room for fear or inhibition. He just jumps.

Think about what happens when we die. There is no way to test the water at that moment. You can't stick your toe in to see what death feels like. All you can do is let go, jump in, and learn to swim.

As a priest, I often watch as the dying wait and wait. Hospice workers will come in and tell us a person has only a few hours left. I rush to do last rites before it's too late. But often, the person will linger for days, weeks, even months. They wait because they are not yet ready to jump.

Those who know that Jesus waits on the other shore, those who can almost see his face, they have an easier time letting go. Of course they do. They know where they are going.

DAY 9 The Miracle of Failure

About an hour later, still another man kept insisting, "Surely this man also was with him, for he is a Galilean." But Peter said, "Man, I do not know what you are talking about!" At that moment, while he was still speaking, the cock crowed. The Lord turned and looked at Peter. Then Peter remembered the word of the Lord, how he said to him, "Before the cock crows today, you will deny me three times." And he went out and wept bitterly. (Luke 22:59–62)

Peter really messed up. He abandoned Jesus and then had the cowardice to deny that he even knew his master. Peter completely fails. He gets a royal "F" when it comes to sticking it out with the greatest teacher he ever had.

How incredible it is that this failure of a disciple should become the greatest leader in the early church. Peter's failure to remain faithful to God brought him face-to-face with the forgiveness of the resurrected Christ. And there is nothing that can change a person like true forgiveness.

One of my favorite movies is *Australia* with Nicole Kidman and Hugh Jackman. Two beautiful people fall in love in the heart of the Outback, but the man, Grover, does not fully appreciate his love for the woman. She urges him to stop his roving, but Grover feels suffocated. Why is she demanding so much of him? He decides to leave her, not knowing if she will take him back.

World War II explodes on the scene and after a terrible bombing, Grover thinks that his love is dead. He is overwhelmed with grief. For the first time in his life, he recognizes how much he loves her, and he is devastated. He knows he has made a terrible mistake.

The despair that Peter experienced after his betrayal caused him to understand the depth of his love and devotion. The fact that God gave him another chance was so wonderful that he was no longer afraid of anything. He could face death without fear from that point on.

Instead of beating yourself up when you make big mistakes, give thanks and ask God to teach you from your failures. Lessons learned from mistakes are powerful lessons. The greater the failure, the greater the possible recovery. (Or, as my fifth grader notes, "You will never forget how to spell the word that you got wrong at the spelling bee.")

God does some of the best work in us when we make a mess of things. God's divinity shines best when we recognize our humanity. Failure provides a great opportunity for us to glimpse the forgiveness of God, and realize what is most important.

Just Do It

Jesus said to Simon Peter, "Simon son of John, do you love me more than these?" He said to him,"Yes, Lord; you know that I love you." Jesus said to him, "Feed my lambs." (John 21:15)

On the shore of the Sea of Galilee, the resurrected Christ has the most incredible conversation with Peter. Jesus asks him, "Do you love me?" He asks three times, frustrating Peter who is exasperated by the repetition of such a simple and obvious question. But Jesus asks three times for a reason. With each answer, Peter is undoing his three denials. Each affirmation of love erases the past sins of Peter, who denied God out of fear. The love of Christ replaces his fear and changes Peter forever.

When Peter answers yes, Jesus gives him one simple and eternal command: "Feed my lambs."

There comes a point in the spiritual journey when you realize that your life is no longer your own. The illusion that you were created simply to enjoy yourself no longer makes sense. If we love God, then our way forward is simple. We must feed the sheep.

Who are the sheep and who are the lambs? They are every human and creature that we encounter in this life. We must care for them all. And that is a tall order.

A few weeks ago, I saw a message on my cell phone. A young mom who is a drug addict had called to ask for help with her rent. Her newborn baby was in the hospital withdrawing from methadone.

I did not want to return the call. All I felt was anger toward her, for bringing a beautiful child into the world and giving him such pain by taking drugs during her pregnancy.

What does it mean to feed her? It does not mean that I hand her cash whenever she asks. It does not mean that I ignore her either. With dread, I called her back and we began to talk.

Feed my sheep, says the resurrected Christ. Feed even those who make you angry and those who never show gratitude. Feed the hungry and those who really don't need your nourishment. When Jesus instructed Peter, he didn't offer a limiting definition of "sheep."

It is such a simple command. But to follow these words takes every ounce of our energy and resources. It is the job of a lifetime.

Day 11 Fishing for People

As he walked by the Sea of Galilee, he saw two brothers, Simon, who is called Peter, and Andrew, his brother, casting a net into the sea—for they were fishermen. And he said to them, "Follow me, and I will make you fish for people." (Matthew 4:18–19)

My grandfather was the quietest, most gentle man. He used to make his grandchildren lie on the floor and he would say "Stiff as a board! Stiff as a board!" Then he would place his gentle old hands behind our little shoulders and lift us up to a standing position, tilting us like a board. At first we would giggle and squirm, and he might make it worse by tickling us. But sooner or later, we would learn how to be stiff as a board and he would move us forward and up.

My grandfather became a fisherman in his old age. He retired to Sanibel Island, Florida, mainly so that he could fish. He parked his small boat in a little cove and every morning he would putter out to sea.

One day, my little brother Jonathan decided to go with Grandpa on a fishing expedition. Jonathan was about five and made a formal request to fish. I remember how Grandpa's eyes shone with pure pleasure at the prospect.

They got in the boat early that morning. We expected that they would not come back until lunch. But by 9 a.m. we heard the puttering motor of the boat entering the small cove near Grandpa's house, and we heard another sound: the sobs of a little boy.

My mother and I rushed outside. Jonathan was weeping but he did not seem hurt. He just kept pointing to the fish, lying dead in the pail. "It couldn't breathe!" he gasped.

Grandpa got out of the boat. He was clearly quite disappointed and a little angry. But in his simple, gentle way, he said, "I don't think I've got a fisherman here."

Jonathan became a vegetarian from that day forward. That lasted about five years. He also refused to speak to Grandpa for the rest of the vacation. Evidently, fishing turned out to be much more violent than Jonathan had thought.

Jesus said to his disciples, "Come to me, and I will make you fish for people."

There is no denying that fishing is a violent act. A fish is swimming along, content in a watery world. And all of a sudden, it is yanked into another dimension. In this new realm, it has to die and give its body for the nourishment of others. It flails around helplessly, its mouth and gills pumping, hoping to find water again, but it finds emptiness, air. It is completely lost, out of its element. Until it is caught, a fish does not even know that it is a creature of water. It has virtually no awareness of water until it is taken out.

I don't think we really contemplate what Jesus meant when he said, "I will make you fish for people." He was talking about yanking people out of their comfortable lives into another level of existence, a new perspective.

A lot of us like to think that we should spread the gospel in order to make people happy, to help them lead content lives. We tell people about Jesus so that they can feel better, so they can get their lives in order. What an appealing thought. Sometimes I wish I could promise people that their lives *will* be easier if they become Christians and practice the faith. But I would not be telling the truth.

In reality when we talk about Jesus to others, we are introducing them to the one who will turn their lives upside down, the one who will ask them to give up everything, even their own lives, out of love and devotion to him. We are yanking them out of their comfortable lives into a realm in which they have little control, in which God alone has the last word.

A friend of mine has six children, and she agreed to provide foster care to a little girl from Afghanistan. This little girl had a severe heart condition and, through the efforts of a local charity, money had been raised to fly her to Jacksonville to have surgery. The little Afghan girl could not walk more than ten steps without becoming short of breath.

Her surgery was much more complex than the doctors had foreseen. The little girl's family was contacted in Afghanistan. She needed to stay in the hospital for three months. And when she was released, she needed to stay in Jacksonville for three more months for medical care. My friend kept in close contact with her mother in Afghanistan.

As the little girl grew in strength, the host family took her to Disneyworld, where she was able to run and play for the first time in her life. My friend took pictures and sent them to Afghanistan. It was a miracle to see her play!

Finally, the little girl was ready to go home. They filled her suitcases with new clothes and gifts for her family, marveling at the good work that God had done through the doctors. They had saved her life.

A few weeks after her arrival in Afghanistan, my American friends got a phone call. The little girl had died.

No one knows what happened, but she had become sick upon her return, and her anxious parents put her in the hospital in Afghanistan. Someone made some mistake, something went terribly wrong. And her precious life was over.

Back in the United States, my friend was devastated. How had this happened? How could God have made this girl better only to take her life back at home?

The Afghan mother called again. "I am calling to say thank you," she said. "My daughter may not have lived long, but, because of you, she ran and played. Because of you, she really lived."

I wish that I could tell you that fishing for people would make everybody happier, but sometimes living a life of sacrifice and learning to love God is like entering another universe, where so much is expected of you and you have so little control. You flail around, doing the best you can, offering your life for something much larger than yourself. You wake up to the fact that there is so much more to life than you can ever comprehend and sometimes the best outcome is the one that you least expected.

We do not follow Jesus to be happy. We follow Jesus to be saved. We follow Jesus because there is so much more to life than just being comfortable. We follow Jesus because we get to taste eternity in him and there is joy there, much better than happiness, there is joy.

After Peter was caught by the great fisherman, he would go on to spread the gospel far and wide. He would be killed for his belief, but I bet, if you asked him, Peter would remember the day that Jesus walked by, the day that he was caught by the Lord, and he would give thanks for the gift of serving God. I believe that Peter would say that it was the best thing that ever happened to him, because the gospel is about so much more than being happy. It is about being caught by Jesus, belonging to him, and what that means for our souls. It is about a life far beyond our existence here. It is about joy. It is about something greater than this life. It is about eternal life.

DAY 12 Comfort Food

While in their joy they were disbelieving and still wondering, he said to them, "Have you anything here to eat?" They gave him a piece of broiled fish, and he took it and ate it in their presence.

(Luke 24:41–43)

When Jesus appeared to the disciples in the Gospel of Luke, he appeared so suddenly that he scared them half to death. Instead of knocking on the door, or walking in like a normal human being, Jesus just pops in. He seemed to have forgotten about normal entrances. And the disciples were startled. Who was this? How did he appear out of thin air? Where did he come from? Was he a ghost?

We are afraid of what we cannot understand. Naturally, the disciples were afraid of the resurrected Christ. Even Peter was speechless.

Jesus is always so straightforward, even after death. He simply addressed the elephant in the room and asked his followers, "Why are you scared?"

Jesus could not understand their fear. He was simply coming to the ones he loved. What could be scary about that?

The disciples seemed mute when it came to describing their fear, so Jesus did something so commonplace that is was deeply reassuring.

He asked them, "Do you have anything to eat?"

And they gave him a piece of fish, just like they always did.

They must have spent day after day eating fish together with Jesus. After all, many of them were fishermen.

We're talking here about comfort food. When I am hungry and tired, emotionally drained or sad, I make myself a peanut butter and jelly sandwich. The familiarity of the taste makes me feel better. I don't know how to explain it. It just does.

The resurrected Jesus ate the fish right in front of them, as he had done countless times before. In doing so, he showed them that he was still Jesus, the guy they loved, their friend and master. He was still the man who had walked with them by the sea and ate fish, cooked over a fire, day in and day out. He was not a ghost. He was flesh and blood. And he wanted to eat.

I was at a meeting where Bishop Edward Konieczny of Oklahoma told a story about his childhood. When he was a very little boy, his mother became violently ill. The bishop did not say what kind of illness took her, but he said that there were times, more than once, when his mother had to be rushed to the hospital. The women of their small Episcopal church would come to his house in the middle of the night, and they would care for him and his brother, fix them something to eat, tell them that everything was going to be OK, and tuck them into bed.

When the world felt like it was caving in, these women would come and offer comfort, and food. And in doing so, they would fill the emptiness and fear with their love. It is no wonder that when he grew up, Edward devoted his life to the church. Sharing food is so simple, and yet so important. Think of how after almost every funeral, we eat so much. We find nothing more comforting than sitting down to a good meal with those we love. In breaking bread together, we find reassurance, security, comfort. Jesus shared food with the disciples at the Last Supper, and then when he appeared in the resurrected form, he ate with them again. Jesus knew his disciples felt frightened and alone after his death. He calmed them by simply asking for something to eat. And in this way, he drew them into the miracle and reality of his resurrection.

Eating is one way we all have of savoring life, for food is needed to sustain life. To eat with another person is to celebrate life itself.

The Ultimate Absolution

Peter addressed the people, "You Israelites, why do you wonder at this, or why do you stare at us, as though by our own power or piety we had made him walk?" (Acts 3:12)

Peter loved Jesus. He loved him so much that he could not be separated from him. He followed him everywhere.

Whenever Jesus escaped alone to a mountain to pray, Peter and the disciples would go searching for Jesus. When they found him, they would scold Jesus for worrying them, like the neurotic parents of an adult child. They simply could not let Jesus out of their sight.

So it is hard to believe that Peter said these words: "I do not know the man."

On the night before Jesus' crucifixion, when all seemed lost and the soldiers had come to take Jesus away, Peter denied him. Not just once, but three times. Peter was afraid and Peter failed. He failed miserably. After all his devotion to and time spent with Jesus, when Peter felt personally threatened, he ran and hid. He left his master alone to die.

I cannot imagine the agony Peter experienced after his denial. The scripture says that he broke down and wept. I can just picture it, a burly fisherman falling to his knees in the dark courtyard in Jerusalem, crying his eyes out, crying because he had failed.

Judas also failed Jesus by selling his friendship for gold and leading the soldiers to capture Jesus. But there is a crucial difference between Peter and Judas. When Peter failed, he did not despair. He waited. He faced his pain and his failure. Judas despaired and took his own life.

I have always believed that Jesus would have forgiven Judas, that even now Jesus waits an eternity to break bread with Judas. But Judas could not trust that forgiveness, not in this life.

Failure is not something to fear. Failure can be a great instrument of resurrection and forgiveness, especially if the one who fails speaks the truth and admits mistakes. To God, failure looks a lot like a teacher. It is something from which we can learn. Failure is not the antithesis of resurrection. Rather, the antithesis of resurrection is despair.

Peter truly learns from his failure. When Jesus rises, and loves Peter once more, Peter becomes a new man. His failure and God's forgiveness forge him into a leader. He becomes truly great.

After the resurrection, Peter is like a new man. In the Book of Acts, he has confidence. He is a true leader. He is articulate and faithful and he never falters. He performs miracles and escapes from prison. Peter becomes a hero.

All this is possible because Peter experienced the miracle of the resurrected Christ. Once he knew that Christ lived, he had no more fear. And there was nothing that he could not do. He had power and he was clear that this power came from God alone.

In one of the poorest neighborhoods in Jacksonville, there is tiny church. It is called St. Mary's. For thirty years, a laywoman has been the vicar of this church. She spends her days among the mentally ill and the drug-addicted. Her name is Sue.

One morning, Sue came into church to find a young man waiting for her. Daniel was mentally ill, a large man in his thirties. Sue had known him and loved him for years. He was homeless at the time and he carried a beer can.

"Now, Daniel, you know not to bring that in here," Sue said. She took the beer can and threw it in the trash. Daniel snapped.

He punched her in the face, then took out a knife, pushed her to her knees and, standing behind her, he held the knife to her neck.

Sue would later recall that she immediately felt a tremendous sense of peace, as if the presence of God was all around her. She said gently and slowly, "Daniel, I love you. Daniel, don't do this. Daniel, I love you."

She kept repeating over and over that she loved him. Daniel's hand began to shake. Finally, he stood her up and turned her around to face him. Then he put his head on her shoulder and wept.

As the police came and took him away, Sue kept asking them to treat Daniel well. She had to go to the emergency room for her bruised face, which took weeks to heal. She spent months afterward in the courts fighting for Daniel to be put in a mental institution rather than prison.

Where did Sue's power and confidence come from? How could she be so calm in such a terrifying situation? Sue knows the risen Christ and she is not afraid of dying. Like Peter, her faith gives her great courage. It gives her great strength.

Early Morning

Then he led them out as far as Bethany, and, lifting up his hands, he blessed them. While he was blessing them, he withdrew from them and was carried up into heaven. (Luke 24:50–51)

Before he ascended into heaven, the risen Christ gathered his disciples together and did something incredibly important, something that we have forgotten how to do. Jesus blessed them.

The Hebrew word for blessing is barak. It literally means "to kneel before someone." It means to spiritually empower another, to say to them, "I want you to prosper in every area of your life." It is the opposite of to curse or cripple someone. To bless is to empower a person to thrive spiritually, socially, physically, emotionally, and in every other way.

In biblical times, it was understood that every person had the power to bless. A father's blessing for his grown son was incredibly powerful. Remember how Jacob and Esau fought over their father's blessing? Jesus also understood the power of a blessing.

Jesus intended for Peter and the disciples to be spiritual leaders. He told Peter, "Whatever you bind on earth will be bound in heaven. Whatever you loose on earth will be loosed in heaven." Jesus directed Peter to bless others, to lead people to God. And Jesus calls us to do the same.

Have you blessed your children? Have you physically placed your hands on their heads and blessed them? Do you realize you have the power to do so? Have you blessed your spouse? What about your parents? Jesus asks this of you. He has blessed you and he sends you out to bless the world.

I've been reading *The Power of a Parent's Blessing* by Craig Hill. He provides interesting information about two American families dating back two hundred years.

Max Jukes was an atheist who married a nonbeliever. From him, 560 descendants were traced; 310 died paupers, 150 became criminals, 7 murderers, 100 were known as drunkards and half the women were prostitutes. The descendants of Max Jukes cost the U.S. government more than 1.25 million nineteenth-century dollars.

Jonathan Edwards was a contemporary of Max Jukes. He was a Christian who practiced his faith with strength. He was known to have blessed his children. He had 1,394 descendants, of whom 295 graduated from college, 13 became college presidents, and 65 college professors. Three were elected U.S. Senators, three were governors, and others were sent as ministers to foreign countries, 30 were judges, 100 were lawyers, one was dean of a law school, 56 were physicians, one was dean of a medical school, 75 were officers in the military, 100 were missionaries, preachers, and prominent authors, 80 held public office, including three mayors of large cities. One was comptroller of the U.S. Treasury and another was vice president of the United States.

I know, there are a lot of factors to consider here—genetics, environment, etc. And certainly many good and faithful people are descendents of nonbelievers, including myself. But Jonathan Edwards blessed his children. He blessed them when they were born, when they reached puberty, when they married. Over and over again, he blessed them.

And you are called to bless, to teach, to heal, just like Jesus. It is time for you to accept your God-given gifts and work to usher in the kingdom of God.

Week 3

....

The Disciples

DAY 15 How to Feast

Jesus said to them again, "Peace be with you. As the Father has sent me, so I send you." When he had said this, he breathed on them. (John 20:21–22)

Not long ago, I had a chance to talk with Bishop N. T. Wright, former archbishop of Durham, about how difficult it is for us to celebrate the entire season of Easter.

"It is true!" he said. "We do not know how to sustain the Great Fifty Days. I have been trying to figure out how to feast the way we should for years during this season.

One year, I insisted on serving champagne for breakfast every morning at my house during the fifty days of Easter. My children thought that I had gone mad."

His point is well taken. How can we feast for fifty days? Part of a feast or a party is its specialness. A celebration is something that surprises us, something unique and full of pleasure. If we feast too much, won't it become mundane, just a part of life? How can we keep the joy in a feast that lasts so long?

When we think of feasting, Americans think of overeating, drinking alcohol, or doing some other things that, if continued for fifty days, would hurt our bodies and perhaps our minds. We think that discipline is the antithesis of the feast, so feasting must mean an end to all discipline. Does it follow that if Lent is about discipline, then Easter is about ignoring discipline?

Notice that when Jesus appears in the resurrected form, he

often gives his friends and disciples assignments. He breathes on them and tells them to go to work for him. He does not say, "Go and stuff yourselves silly!" Instead, he says, "Now you are mine. Do as I do."

What if we sustained the feast by making someone else happy each of the fifty days? Joy tends to multiply. It is unique and incredible in that way. Give it away and more fills your heart, until it is overflowing. Joy cannot be found in indulging in pleasurable activities until they are devoid of all pleasure. A good song is not meant to be played over and over until you are sick of it. Instead, all good things are meant to be given away. And the best way to sustain the joy of Easter is to give away the best thing of all, the news about Jesus and his resurrection.

DAY 16 To the Ones Who Showed Up

Now it was Mary Magdalene, Joanna, Mary the mother of James, and the other women with them who told these things to the apostles. But these words seemed to them an idle tale, and they did not believe them. (Luke 24:10–11)

When the women returned after talking with the angels at the tomb of Jesus, they tried to explain the resurrection to the disciples. And their words sounded like pure nonsense. The disciples could not believe them.

After all, if Jesus wanted to prove that he was alive, why did he reveal himself to women first? Women were not even considered human. They were generally not educated, or trusted. This sure didn't seem like a brilliant strategy. If Jesus wanted to make his resurrection known to the world, why had he chosen women as eyewitnesses?

Perhaps Jesus did not come to prove anything. Maybe he rose from the dead to show his love and forgiveness for all of us. And the ones who came to the tomb saw him first. He simply came to those who looked for him.

What a wild idea it is that we might get to see God simply because we go looking. Experiencing God is not some kind of reward for the best behaved or the most articulate among us. God comes to those of us who are willing to search for a way to make sense of it all. God comes to the ones who continue to risk trying again even after their hearts have been broken.

A teenage boy went to visit the grave of his older brother. His brother was killed late one evening when he pulled over to the side of the road and tried to help a woman who had been in a car accident. He crossed the road to help her and was hit. It was like the murder of a Good Samaritan. It made no sense. The boy's parents were devastated. The only thing that kept them alive was the presence of their other son, the younger brother.

You would think that a boy of fourteen would not want to visit a graveyard. You would think that he would be busy hanging out with friends or playing video games. But he chose to go to the grave. And he laid a wreath of flowers there.

The younger brother posted his visit to the graveyard on Facebook. He took a picture of the flowers that he had placed on his brother's grave. He wrote of the strange peace that he felt.

The resurrection strangely comes in moments like this one, to someone who does not run away, but stares death straight in the eye and looks beyond, in hope of seeing something more.

God Had Love in Mind

Then beginning with Moses and all the prophets,
he interpreted to them the things about himself in
all the scriptures. (Luke 24:27)

I have been married for fifteen years. I was so blessed to find JD, my husband. I never could have imagined finding a man more suited to who I am and the person I want to become. I thank God every day for him.

Before I met JD, I spent a lot of wasted time worrying about the person I would marry. I was concerned that any man who would want to marry me would probably be a bore. I couldn't imagine spending my entire adult life with a boring person. This thought really troubled me.

Well, JD is anything but boring. And what I have learned is that God had a love story in mind for me, one that I could not have chosen myself. I didn't even have a clue about what love could be. But God had love in mind from the beginning, before I even knew what it really looked like. God knew more about what I needed than I knew myself.

The experience of the church is something like that.

The first fully documented liturgy of the early Christian church took place in about 150 AD on the night before Easter. It lasted all night, for it was a way of reminding us that God had Jesus in mind for us from the very beginning.

For forty days during Lent, people who wanted to become Christians had to study and fast. They were separated from the body of the church. They read and they prayed. Then on the eve of Easter, they got ready for the biggest celebration of their lives.

They were called catechumens, those about to become Christian. They wore white, like brides. All through the night, the early church members read to them from the Hebrew scriptures, by the light of the Pascal candle. All through the night, they heard the history of how the Hebrew people had waited, longing for a messiah to save them. They heard about Adam and Eve, about how Abraham offered his son Isaac for sacrifice, about how their people escaped from slavery in Egypt, about how Elijah had a vision of dry bones rising to become bodies, of flesh and sinew. And as they heard these ancient texts, the people realized once more how God had love in mind for them from the beginning. In spite of that experience, they had no idea what a true messiah would look like. But God knew and when they were ready, God revealed the ways in which that love had been at work from the beginning.

When all the readings were over, just as the sun was about to rise, the early Christians baptized the catechumens. And as the waters of baptism poured over the heads of the new believers, the sun rose and with the coming of the dawn, the church celebrated the resurrection of Jesus, shouting and dancing for joy.

We had no idea what love in all its fullness looked like until Jesus came. Once he came, everything acquired a new dimension. The pieces of the puzzle finally came together, and we realized that God had love in mind for us from the very beginning.

DAY 18 Walking to Emmaus

While they were talking and discussing, Jesus himself came near and went with them, but their eyes were kept from recognizing him. (Luke 24:15)

When I am trying to make a difficult decision, I often like to go for a walk. I find this a good way to process, to let the fresh air in and to move my limbs. It helps me think.

I believe the same is true of the two disciples who left for Emmaus after the crucifixion. So much had happened and they just needed to think, so they set off, hoping that the motion of their legs and the air rushing through their lungs would give them some kind of perspective, some way to understand.

When Jesus approached them on the road, they did not recognize him. They were so wrapped up in trying to make sense of it all, they could not see clearly. They were not looking. How often do we do this? We get so wrapped up in the problems of life that we cannot see the solutions when they are right beside us. We become more invested in analyzing our challenges than in actually solving them.

The risen Christ did not identify himself to them. Instead, he walked along with them. He talked to them about scripture, helping them understand the tragic events of the past few days. He urged them to see a larger purpose involved.

"Oh, fools and slow of heart to believe all that the prophets have spoken! Ought Christ not to have suffered these things and then entered his glory?" Jesus scolds them for not looking at the big picture, for not searching the scripture with an eye for guidance. He is not easy on them. He does not coddle them but tells them to get back to their studies. In their grief, they are not seeing God's plan.

Together, the disciples and Jesus remembered the events in scripture that foretold of one who would come and suffer for us. Jesus helped them unveil all that they had once learned. The disciples seemed to grow more energized as he explained everything to them. It was as if they moved from despair to hope and they didn't even realize who he was!

I marvel at the patience of this one who rose from the dead. It is amazing that he did not just say, "It is me! Everything will be OK!" Instead he walked with them in their pain and confusion and guided them as they found their own way back into the light. He did not solve their pain, he helped them make sense of it. It was only after they had found their way to hope that he revealed who he really was.

Lately, I have come to imagine that Jesus walks beside me guiding my thoughts toward good news. He does not hand me answers. He shows patience. He walks with me, listening, redirecting, and guiding me to find my way through the mess and confusion of life. Of course he must do it this way. How else would I learn?

DAY 19 Listening

> *Some Saducees, those who say there is no resurrection, came to him and asked him a question, "Teacher, Moses wrote for us that if a man's brother dies, leaving a wife but no children, the man shall marry the widow and raise up children for his brother. Now there were seven brothers; the first married, and died childless; then the second and the third married her, and so in the same way all seven died childless. Finally, the woman also died. In the resurrection, therefore, whose wife will the woman be? For the seven had married her." (Luke 20:27–33)*

Why did Jesus appear to the disciples, but to none of the Pharisees or Saducees? These were deeply devout men. They were curious about heaven and about the resurrection. Why did they not come to know the resurrected Christ? And why was Jesus so deeply critical of them?

In her book *Time to Think*, Nancy Kline remembers what her mother told her as she lay dying:

> *The day before she died, my mother said a startling thing to me. "I apologize," she said, "for the mess my generation has imposed upon yours. I wish I could have left you a better legacy. I just hope I have left you a measure*

of courage to face what we have done, and a
measure of hope to do something about it."[1]

Nancy thought a lot about her mother's words. Her mother never had a job outside the home. She never went to war. She just raised Nancy and her siblings. But her mother had one great gift. Her mother knew how to listen.

Nancy writes about how she would come home from school, and her mother would sit at the kitchen table with her and eagerly listen as Nancy recounted her day. She did not just want to hear the events of the day. What she really got excited about were Nancy's ideas. She wanted to hear what Nancy thought about everything, as if Nancy's thoughts mattered. And, as a result, Nancy grew up with the rare ability to think for herself. When everyone else was just trying to fit in, Nancy was thinking. She became a professor. And she has spent her life researching the act of listening itself.

Nancy believes that the act of listening itself can change the world. She believes that when we stop everything we are doing and give our undivided attention to another person, without judgment and without criticism, and try with all our might to truly hear the thoughts of the individual in front of us, the listener unleashes a great power in the speaker. And when that person is heard, he or she begins to feel safe to truly think deeply.

When someone truly listens to another person, a sacred space is created. In the language of scripture, one could say the Logos, the word of God itself, enters the conversation,

1. Nancy Kline, *Time to Think: Listening to Ignite the Human Mind* (London: Castle Illustrated, 1999), 14.

and extraordinary things can happen. Often the one who speaks has some kind of a revelation, if someone is really listening.

Before his death, Jesus roundly and unabashedly criticizes the leaders of the synagogue to his disciples. I always get a little nervous when I read this. After all, as a priest, I wear robes. I parade around. I like to talk. Was it the robes that made Jesus mad? Was it the words? Was it the fact that these religious leaders got paid?

I think that what made Jesus furious with the scribes and the Pharisees was very simple. They did not listen. They were all about themselves. Their hearts were not open to God or to anyone else. They spoke prayers, but they did not listen.

When you think of it, Jesus did an awful lot of listening. When the crowds thronged around him and they brought suffering to him, before Jesus healed, he always listened. He asked people what they wanted. When he looked at a person, he truly saw them, whether it was the rich young man or the poor widow. He saw directly into the heart of a person. And it was this that changed lives as much as the healing itself.

Some of the greatest learning experiences I have had have been in the office of a therapist or spiritual director. Good therapy is worth the money. When I was in my early twenties, I went to see a therapist who was very kind. I was in a lot of pain at the time and I sat and cried in his office for about three straight months. It took even longer for me to look up and notice the objects in his office.

He was so attentive, so quiet. He would sometimes ask a simple question or just smile at me. After about six months, I was babbling about something when he interrupted me. I was annoyed that he would bust in on my monologue, but he simply said, "Kate, I'm sorry to interrupt, but look out the window." There was this beautiful buck staring in at us. He had huge antlers and he just stood there. I was dumbstruck.

About ten years later, I returned to Connecticut for a visit and decided to go to see this wonderful man and thank him for his listening. We sat in his office once more. I asked him if he remembered seeing the buck and he said, "Oh, yes. But do you remember what you were talking about at the time?"

"I have no idea," I said. "I was just babbling on about something."

"No," he said. "You were saying that you felt called to the priesthood, but you wished that God would give you a sign that he wanted this of you. You just wished God would give you a sign."

I'm afraid that I began to cry again. I cried because God was listening. But I also cried because this old man had listened and he never forgot. He listened to me when I had stopped listening to myself.

Perhaps one way of resurrecting the Great Feast of Easter is simply to listen to just one person. Sit still. Don't let your eyes wander. Don't speak much. Don't overwhelm the person with questions, as the Saducees did to Jesus. Just take a genuine interest in someone and really work to listen. Listening to others is good practice, for when you can listen to others, you can listen to God. In fact, many times God will speak to you through others.

God bless those Saducees and Pharisees. They thought so much about themselves that they did not listen. They forgot that God acts most powerfully when the Logos has room to be heard, when we quiet down and make room for someone else to be wiser than we are. That is when great things happen.

DAY 20 Leaving the Tomb

He has been raised; he is not here. . . . He is going ahead of you to Galilee. (Mark 16:6–7)

When the disciples came looking for Jesus, they found an empty tomb. It must have been dark and dismal in that space, where Jesus no longer was. The angels that met them at the tomb told them that Jesus had gone and that he was heading into Galilee. The disciples were to follow him there.

In order to experience the resurrection, the disciples had to leave the darkness and emptiness, believing that Jesus could be found in the light of day, in the beautiful hills of Galilee. If they did not leave the tomb, if they had stayed there weeping and disbelieving, they would have never seen the risen Christ. In other words, when they came looking for death, they found emptiness and a promise that they could find Jesus somewhere else.

It is deeply significant that it was not Jesus sitting in the tomb. He did not wait in the darkness for them to arrive. He wasted no time moving into the light, and if they wanted to see him, they had to move into the light as well. The darkness and emptiness of the tomb could not contain him.

There are moments in our lives when we must decide if we are going to wallow in darkness and self-pity, or if we are going to step into the light. Suffering is going to come upon all of us, for we live in a broken world. It is what we do with the suffering that determines how we experience resurrection.

Years ago, one of my parishioners became pregnant

with her third child. The baby was diagnosed with Down syndrome in utero. She came to me at this incredible juncture in her life. She had a choice of whether to see this child as a blessing or as someone who brought her pain and work. She chose to see the little one as a blessing. This child was a gift from God.

The baby, a little girl, was born into the loving arms of the entire church. That year, at the Christmas pageant, she was our Christ child. We all sat in the congregation watching Mary hold this tiny, helpless infant with Down syndrome and we saw the risen Christ. There was not a dry eye in the place.

Have you decided to leave the tomb and search for the risen one? It is dark in the tomb, but it feels safe. The light can be scary. It can blind us. But we cannot experience the resurrection if we don't leave the tomb.

DAY 21 Burning Hearts

"Were not our hearts burning within us while he was talking to us on the road, while he was opening the scriptures to us?" (Luke 24:32)

Two disciples were walking on the road to Emmaus from Jerusalem. One of them was named Cleopas, the other is not named. (I have always wondered if this second disciple was a woman and her name was omitted for that reason. Perhaps she was Cleopas' wife.)

I believe that Cleopas and his companion needed to process the incredible tragedy of Jesus' death and the rumors they had heard about his appearances. This news was too much to take sitting down. They had to get up and walk.

As they were walking, a stranger approached. The stranger kindly asked them what they were talking about and, like clients with a trusted therapist, the disciples just let it all spill out. They poured out their worries, their heartache, and their hope.

Then the stranger showed them that all that had happened really did make sense. By recounting the events of scripture, the stranger showed them that they were not crazy, but that all they had experienced had happened by design, that all this mess was really part of a greater plan.

The disciples would later recall that their hearts "burned within them" as the stranger spoke. Like a bell that is struck, the truth of his words resonated in their hearts, sounding deep within, and setting everything straight. All the pieces of chaos and disorder, of pain and confusion came together. Like pieces of a puzzle, they began to fit.

I believe that experiences of the heart are indicators of the presence of God. We cannot see God or touch God, but we can feel God's presence when our hearts soar. When you are moved by beautiful music, God is present. When you see a beautiful sunset that takes your breath away, God is present. When you have struggled for months with a relationship that is broken, and suddenly you are able to forgive and find peace, God is present.

Pay attention to the movement of your heart. It is the best sign we have that God is walking beside us.

Week 4

....

Paul

DAY 22 The Five Hundred

For I handed on to you as of first importance what I in turn received: that Christ died for our sins in accordance with the scriptures, and that he was buried, and that he was raised on the third day in accordance with the scriptures, and that he appeared to Cephas, then to the twelve. Then he appeared to more than five hundred brothers and sisters at one time, most of whom are still alive, though some have died. (1 Corinthians 15:3–6)

There is only one mention in the Bible of the five hundred people who saw the resurrected Christ. We have no details as to who they were. Had they known Jesus before he died? Had they professed any belief in him at all or even curiosity? Did they know who he was when he appeared? By the time that Paul wrote his first letter to the Corinthian church, some of these five hundred witnesses had died, though most of them were still alive. Who were they?

The mysterious five hundred will never be identified. Even Paul was not with them when they witnessed the resurrected Christ. And Paul goes on to say that Christ appeared to him as well, though he did not see Christ's body, but only heard his voice and saw a light. This brief mention of five hundred witnesses is perhaps a gift to us, because we can consider ourselves like them. We can pray that we might too catch glimpses of the resurrected Christ.

How do you know when you are having an experience of the risen Christ? Paul's encounter was so powerful it blinded him. He was changed forever and he did not have a doubt that it was God who had changed him. Most of us do not have experiences of God that are so spectacular; rather we wade about in the murky waters of discernment and contemplation, hoping for some kind of powerful encounter.

Mother Teresa of Calcutta loved God and felt God's presence for years. Then that assurance of God's presence went away and she was left in a state of emptiness. She continued her ministry to the poor without pausing at all, but her diaries reveal a deep sadness and hunger for Christ. That void remained for the rest of her life. She felt the pain of Christ's absence.

The yearning for God's presence is in fact a sign of that presence. Why do we long to see the resurrected Christ if there is not a part of us that is meant for it? We want to see someone whom we love and whose presence we have experienced on some level. I do not long to see someone who has no impact on my life. Yearning for God is a sign that I already love God and, in fact, know God. The desire for God tells us that in fact we are already in a relationship.

DAY 23 **Seeing with the Eyes of the Heart**

With the eyes of your heart enlightened . . .
(Ephesians 1:18)

Jesus had great insight. He was able to see right into people and know them. He loved with a kind of clarity and resourcefulness that was uncanny. He told people what he knew they needed to hear and he knew that there was more to this earth than what we can see physically.

Years ago, a woman in my church had a dream. It was a vision, really, of heaven. The colors were so vibrant, so beautiful, that they seared themselves into her memory. She would never forget that glimpse of beauty. Never. But she was afraid to tell people what she had seen. It changed her life. She started going to church and praying. She felt a kind of peace that would never leave, but it took her years to get up the courage to tell me about her vision.

"Am I crazy?" she asked.

"No," I said, "you were given a gift. You saw something with the eyes of your heart."

St. Paul describes the heart as having eyes. "With the eyes of your heart enlightened," he says.

When those we love die, we can no longer see them physically. We cannot look at them, touch them, or talk to them. But the eyes of our hearts still see them. They still live inside us and we love them. They are still visible to us in our hearts.

After my father-in-law died, I felt as if I came to know

him even better. As a Methodist pastor, he had been my mentor. In death, he became my saint. I talk to him from time to time, asking for his guidance, his help. And I know that he watches me. I know that he stays with me, helping my husband and me to raise our children, to live better lives.

Life is more than what you can see with your eyes. There is a whole life with God that only the eyes of the heart can see. We must practice seeing with our hearts and not just our minds. Believe in the eternal presence of those who love you, whether they live here or have gone on ahead to God. Believe that their love for you is real and that it is with you even now, at this very moment.

DAY 24 Freedom in Discipline

I die every day! That is certain, brothers and sisters, as my boasting of you—a boast that I make in Christ Jesus my Lord. If with merely human hopes I fought with wild animals at Ephesus, what would I have gained by it? If the dead are not raised, "Let us eat and drink, for tomorrow we die." (I Corinthians 15:31–32)

I stink at exercise. Every morning, I get up and my dog, Ella, an overgrown pup, is already itching to go. I rub my eyes and feel sorry for myself as I get ready to take her on a jog. She pulls like crazy, running me. Most days we run for about twenty minutes at a kind of a slow pace. Some days I just walk fast. The trees and the air wake me up. I begin to give thanks to God for a new day, to pray, maybe let a song run through my head.

Sometimes I see someone coming toward me, another woman my age, who is really running. All of a sudden, I pick up my pace. I throw my shoulders back and try to look strong, as if I'm running for miles and miles. I smile and say hello. Then, once she is out of range, I slog again. I come up with familiar excuses to stop running.

"It's not really that good for you, to pound your body into the pavement."

"There are really fit people who walk."

"Maybe I am just too vain."

"I've done enough."

"I need to be satisfied with the body I have."

"I can't pray well when I am running."

It's all a bunch of hooey, these excuses that run through my mind. I know what this is really about. It's about my spiritual life. My body is a part of my spiritual life. And if I don't manage to take care of my flesh, I won't be able to grow closer to God.

In his letter to the Galatians, Paul talks about the relationship of the flesh and the spirit. We inhabit bodies that God has made, and these bodies are important. But our relationship with God far exceeds the physical. We have a spiritual life that can soar beyond the clouds. The body is holy, it was made by God, but it cannot be all important, or we will never be free to experience God. The body is like a child who must be given boundaries and discipline, or it will distract us completely from God.

If I did exactly what my body wanted, I would lie in bed most of the day. I would eat ice cream by the quart and watch stupid romance movies. But I would become depressed, and I would feel removed from God over time. So I must haul my body out of bed in the morning and run with my hyper dog, not to try to look attractive but to discipline my body so that I can serve God and grow closer to God.

When I lived in Kansas, I joined a gym. There was a woman there who was in her sixties. She began to talk to me while we were on the eliptical machines. She told me she had been a beautiful blonde, just a knock-out in her younger years. Her whole identity had been caught up in her body. She dressed immaculately and was always conscious of what others thought of her appearance. Then she began to age. So she injected her skin with botox. Then came her first real face-lift, then the second. But nothing made her look the way she had when she was young. Now, after multiple surgeries, she looked like a plastic specter of herself. And she realized that something was terribly wrong. She knew there must be more to life than just trying to look good, but she could not escape the slavery that she had created. She was in bondage to her body, exercising madly for hours each day and never satisfied.

Another woman I knew had been hurt by her father at a tender age, and she carried about two hundred pounds of extra fat. She claimed a genetic problem, but every day, she stopped at Krispy Kreme. She had to get her knees replaced. She was in constant pain. She was also a slave to her body.

If you are to truly follow Christ, to be free, Paul is quite clear that you must liberate yourself from your body. And that means, quite simply, learning what is best for you and saying no to what is not. Create a physical rule of life for yourself. Find out what you need to do to care for your body enough that you don't have to think about it all the time. What would it take to liberate you from your body? Whatever that is, do it.

If you want to be a disciple, you also have to travel light. Remember that when Jesus invited someone to follow him, he did not wait around. He did not wait for folks who wanted time to pack. He did not even indulge the man who wanted time to bury his father. He wants you and me and he's not going to wait.

Do you have too much stuff? Too much stuff can create another kind of bondage. Are you enslaved to your home? What do you need to get rid of to liberate yourself? Can you live more simply? Do you even know where all of your belongings are? Do you own items that you haven't used or seen in more than a year? Give them away. Free your soul from too much stuff. When Jesus comes, you don't want to be caught packing.

You cannot begin to truly love God if you are obsessed with your body or your stuff. Your mind needs to be freed from obsessing about these things. Get your priorities straight, and make room for what is most important in your life: God.

Real Love

[Love] believes all things, hopes all things,.
(1 Corinthians 13:7)

There is something innate in us that recognizes authentic love. Even a child who has been abandoned by her parents, a child who has known no affection, can sense when love is inauthentic or ungenuine.

There was a child in my congregation who was angry. His parents were divorced, and his mom moved to a small apartment. He had attention deficit disorder and was unable to sit still in school. His vision was impaired and he struggled without glasses. "My teacher hates me," he told me. And what he meant was that he didn't feel she loved him because of her frustration with him. She did not hate him, but neither did she authentically love him.

When this boy came to church, I was afraid for him. He seemed so angry. He would hit his sisters, act out during services, and he did not want to be baptized. But our parish community loved him. One man became his godfather and took him to Scout meetings. Another parishioner bought his family some clothes. Someone else donated furniture. We just poured out love for him. And he responded like a sponge, absorbing it all. A parishioner took him to get eyeglasses, and another arranged for him to get help with his ADHD.

Now he and his sisters stand with me at the back of the church when I greet people after Sunday services. He hugs me. He sings in our chorister program. He wants to stay at

---

church even after coffee hour is over, and he looks forward to our Wednesday night parish dinners. He is always smiling.

This child was like a plant that was thirsty. As soon as he was watered with authentic, unconditional love, he bloomed. And he recognized love when he met it, despite a childhood full of fear and misunderstanding. It was not so hard to reach him.

How many children have the resurrection life within them, ready to bloom with the slightest bit of encouragement? How many children could be raised up from hopelessness to joy through the simple embrace of a community that adores them? Sometimes I marvel at how much of a difference the church can make in the life of a person. We are the bearers of Christ's love to the world. Once we unleash that potential, there is no telling what we can accomplish.

DAY 26 Your True Self

Now we see in a mirror, dimly, but then we will
see face to face. . . . Then I will know fully, even
as I have been fully known. (1 Corinthians 13:12)

I went to the beach on spring break with my kids. Before we left, I tried on my bathing suit in front of the bedroom mirror. My husband walked in and told me I looked great, but I scoffed. He suggested that I give up looking in the mirror for Lent.

What a good idea, I thought. How much time do I waste wishing that I could look like Kate Middleton or Gwyneth Paltrow? Sometimes I think that women can't even see themselves clearly despite so much time in front of our mirrors, because we are so critical of our bodies. I should hang an icon on my bathroom wall in place of the mirror and look at that. Or, above my mirror, I could tape the quote from Psalm 139 that reads, "I knit you together in your mother's womb. . . . You are wonderful and marvelously made."

When Christ looks at you, he does not see what you see in the mirror. He does not see the wrinkles or the sagging thighs. He does not see fat or thin or ugly or beautiful. He does not see your past or define you by your race or ethnicity. Jesus sees with the eyes of God.

I believe that God sees not what we have been or what we look like now, but God sees all that we can become. In a flash, God sees all that we can be, beyond time, our very best selves. God sees the fullness of who we can be.

When a child is baptized in the Episcopal Church, parents and godparents take vows. The priest asks, "Will you, by your prayers and witness, help this child to grow into *the full stature of Christ?*" And they answer "We will."

I believe that God already knows who that child can become, what the fullness of Christ might look like for that precious human soul.

Both Luke and Jacob, my two older sons, have had growth spurts this year. We have marks on a wall in our kitchen where we record their growth. I am watching as their faces emerge from boyhood, and it is like watching them become the people that God always intended them to be. When they were babies, they were just a fraction of themselves. But from the moment they were born, God knew what they would become. I am just watching, trying to catch up. It is like their true essence is revealed gradually to me every day, just a little bit more.

When we look at others, we must realize we can't see what God sees. We cannot know the depths and the strength of those who seem to us to have lost everything. How can we judge others? We cannot even see ourselves clearly.

It is not just God who is unknown to us. It is not just God who is a great and powerful mystery. We do not even understand ourselves. We do not know all that we can be, all that God hopes and dreams for us to become. Only God can see who we really are. Only God has a resurrection perspective.

DAY 27 Practice

To them God chose to make known how great among the Gentiles are the riches of the glory of this mystery, which is Christ in you, the hope of glory. (Colossians 1:27)

Three times a week, I go to a yoga class where my teacher gently asks our bodies to do things that I never thought were possible. And, thank God, there are no mirrors in the studio. So I try. I try to bend myself. I sweat and struggle and even cry sometimes (especially when beautiful music is playing), and I have discovered something amazing about the human body.

If we keep trying to do something physically demanding, over and over again, we find eventually we are able to do it. It is not that the movement becomes less difficult. It is that our ability increases. Our bodies adapt to the challenge and the challenge shapes us.

Resurrection, according to St. Paul, is not so much about getting to heaven when you die. Rather, it is about allowing Christ to live within you now, to make room for eternal life in your heart. At first, this is awkward and uncomfortable. You see a poor person on the street who asks for help with buying gas for his car and you think, "I don't know this guy from Adam! Why should I take time out of my day and money out of my pocket for him? I need to get home!" It feels awkward and strange to see the world as if God were inside you. At first, you may catch a glimpse of what it would look like to love your neighbor, but you just can't stretch yourself to get there.

But just remember that Christ lives in you, that he was planted there at your baptism, and try to see the world through his eyes. One day, you will be able to do it. One day, you will stretch your soul in service of others and it will begin to shape your very self.

Christ lives in you, nudging you on to love the world with a wild abandon that the world does not deserve. Christ will wake you up at night to pray for someone who is hurting. Christ will call you to your knees for the love of someone who is dying. And the more you simply try, the greater your ability will be to see the world through his eyes.

The desert fathers of the sixth century spent years in silent prayer. They knew that love is not born of warm and fuzzy feelings, love is born simply of practice. It lives inside you. Make room for it to grow and stretch yourself to give everything you have to the one who loves you and made you. Try over and over again and the resurrected Christ will take on new dimensions in your life.

DAY 28 A New Birth

For neither circumcision nor uncircumcision
is anything; but a new creation is everything!
(Galatians 6:15)

Victor turned sixty and felt like his life was over. He was fit and healthy, could still run five miles and eat a good meal, but an indescribable shadow seemed to have descended on his life. He had not accomplished what he hoped to do. He was a nobody, mediocre in his field. He had not been the kind of father he always envisioned he would be.

Early one morning, he awoke and said his prayers, as he had every morning for decades. But today felt different. The sunlight filtered through the blinds and he felt a tinge of hope. A feeling of newness washed over him. He knew this feeling was from God. He was being given another chance.

What does it mean to be born again? Many evangelical Christians use the term as a once-in-a-lifetime experience when you become a believer and you are born to a life with God. But I believe that we can be born over and over and over again.

Each morning, God makes you a new creation. You are given a clean slate, a new canvas. Your life is not defined by your age or what you have or have not accomplished so far. It is defined by this moment and this moment alone. God raises you from the dead and breathes life into your body. You are born again every day.

I remember when I held my first child. He was so new, so pure and innocent. That is how God views us every day. To

God, no one is old or jaded. We are born each moment, over and over again, to the fullness that God intends for us. Such is the nature of God's love.

Week 5

....

John of Patmos

Near

> *Blessed is the one who reads aloud the words of*
> *the prophecy, and blessed are those who hear and*
> *who keep what is written in it; for the time is*
> *near. (Revelation 1:3)*

We hear a lot in the New Testament about the time being near. Jesus will come soon, Paul proclaims. We must all be ready! In the book of Revelation, John of Patmos declares that God will be coming soon to resolve all things.

How do we read these passages two thousand years later? Obviously, in linear, human time, we know Jesus has not yet come back to earth to resolve all pain in a kind of second coming. We are still here. We are still struggling. We are not yet complete. Or are we?

The time is near, John writes. "Near."

Quantum physics gives us some wonderful insight into time itself. According to the physicists, time is the fourth dimension, but there are more dimensions beyond linear time. How numerous are these dimensions? Some physicists say as many as thirteen.

The Greek New Testament uses two words to define time: chronos and kairos. Chronos is linear time, as in the word "chronological." Kairos is God's time, in which many things can happen at once.

There has been a long-standing debate in the church for centuries about resurrection. When exactly will we be raised? Will it be when we die or will it be at the end of all days when Christ comes to earth again?

John said the time is nearly two thousand years ago! Was he just mistaken?

I believe that God's time is different from our own. In God's time, we can be raised at death *and* at the end of days both at once. Both are possible because God exists in dimensions far beyond linear time.

For thousands of years, the church has taught that when we celebrate the Eucharist, we are not just remembering something that happened long ago at the Last Supper, we are actually participating in the event itself. Surrounded by angels and archangels, we exist in kairos time with God. It happened then and it happens now. Christ is near.

Day 30   I Am

I am the Alpha and the Omega. (Revelation 1:8)

We were at a dinner party not long ago. A recently widowed gentleman, Mack, shuffled to his car after the party. He was happy after spending an evening with friends and too inebriated to understand how dangerous it was to get behind the wheel. As JD and I watched him try to back up his car, we realized he could kill himself or someone else if one of us didn't drive him home. JD suggested that I take Mack in his car and JD would follow in our car. Mack was grateful to let me drive.

As I drove Mack home, he became sad, and very talkative. Oh, how he had loved his wife, he told me. He found himself surrounded by her things in their old home and he refused to move when his children pressed him to come live with them. "I am with her there," he said.

The overwhelming loneliness that Mack was experiencing struck me with force. The love of his life, his wife of sixty-two years, had died. He was so alone that he was drinking himself into a stupor. What else could he do?

I carefully pulled the car into his tiny garage. It was a tight fit. Mack could hardly make it up the stairs. And then I left him there, all alone.

God gave us a name to use in referring to the Almighty. And that name is so significant that it sums up the event of Christ's incarnation and it sums up the essence of resurrection itself. In that name, we find north and south, east and west.

In that name, we find both Christmas and Easter. That name is everything and it is so simple.

I AM.

God tells us, over and over again, in so many ways: I AM.

I am with you, always.

I will never leave you.

Death cannot part me from you.

I am resurrection.

I wanted to tell this to Mack in the car. I wanted to yell it out. But he was too drunk to hear me. So he walked into the darkness of his empty house, feeling alone.

But he was not alone.

Saints

After this I looked, and there was a great
multitude that no one could count, from every
nation, from all tribes and peoples and languages,
standing before the throne and before the Lamb,
robed in white, with palm branches in their hands.
(Revelation 7:9)

Bill Tomes was a therapist in a thriving hospital practice. He had been offered a job as an in-house counselor for a big corporation. He did not know whether to accept or not. Struggling with this decision, he passed a Catholic church and saw that the door was open. He felt drawn to enter, though he never went to church. He asked God what he should do. And he heard a voice in his head.

"I'll lead. You follow. All trust. No fear."

Bill did not take the corporate job, and he didn't stay in his old job either. Instead he became a monk. Today, he wears a robe made of patches from his old blue jeans. Every day, he goes out in the streets of Chicago and meets gang members on their turf. He calls them his brothers and they call him Brother Bill. He drives them around in his beat-up old car. He takes them to the movies. When they get into fights with other gangs, he comes to the scene and quietly stands between the rival factions. One time a bullet flew very close to his head. Another time he was hit with a bottle, but he did not move. He stands there, between guys who want to murder each other. He just stands there and loves them.

A saint is a crazy person. Saints do not see the world as we do. They don't think down is down or up is up. They don't think money or worldly goods are important. They are so in love with God that they have returned to Eden. Being a saint is all about perspective. A saint has to fall in love with God totally and stop thinking like this world. As a saint, you have a resurrection heart, a resurrection perspective. You begin to live in Eden again. Often people think you are absolutely crazy. It may take hundreds of years before they realize you are a saint.

Francis was the son of a wealthy cloth merchant, working to sell his father's wares. He saw a man who was hungry. Francis ran after the man and gave him all the money he had made. When his father learned of this, he punished Francis severely. But Francis did not see things as his father saw them. He saw a hungry man and to him nothing else mattered but caring for that man, not money, not his father's expectations, nothing.

Francis saw God in everything. He saw what God wanted and he saw what God made, as if he were already living in heaven. When his father told him to come home, he said no, he was giving his life to God. His father said, "Then give me your belongings." So Francis, in front of the bishop and a crowd of people, took off his clothes. All of them. And he stood naked, like Adam and Eve. He was not at all concerned with what people thought of him. He thought only of God.

When Francis saw a sunset, he would cry tears of joy at its beauty. He spoke to the sun and the moon as if they were his companions. He held the animals and knew that they were precious in God's eyes, valuable and magnificent.

Toward the end of his life, Francis experienced stigmata, wounds in his hands and feet, just like the wounds that pierced Jesus. He did not show them to many people. He mostly hid them, but they were proof of how deeply he felt the pain and joy of Jesus.

Katie Davis is a young woman in her twenties. In high school, she was homecoming queen and class president. But she fell deeply in love with God, like Francis. After graduation, she decided not to go to college, but to move to Uganda. Because of war and HIV/AIDS, there are thousands of orphans in Uganda. Katie simply began to feed them and teach them about God. Then she started adopting orphans. Now she is mother to more than twenty Ugandan children. Is she crazy? Yes! Crazy in love with God.

How much do you love God? Can you be crazy too? Or are you too afraid to let go of your reputation, your money, or your fear? Think of how you care for your pets and how they trust you. Don't you know that God will take care of you too?

Saints live in the resurrection life. They know that they already belong to God.

DAY 32 The Blood of the Lamb

For you were slaughtered and by your blood you ransomed for God saints from every tribe and language and people and nation; you have made them to be a kingdom of priests serving our God. (Revelation 5:9–10)

After initial hesitation, I broke down and bought the best-selling book *The Hunger Games*. It is simply written, fast-paced, and incredibly violent. But I must say, it captivated me to the end. It was the end that fascinated me the most.

The story is about a future in which a demented government has taken over a country and divided it into twelve districts. To keep control of the districts, the government enforces a once-a-year tribute called the Hunger Games. One boy and one girl between the ages of twelve and eighteen are chosen from each of the twelve districts. They are dressed up and paraded before cameras like celebrities, then taken to an amphitheater where the world watches as they are forced to battle one another to the death.

The winning boy and girl are drugged and brought to a kind of treatment facility. By the time the games are over, they are scarred and bloody. The boy has a deep gash in his leg. The girl has a huge cut on her forehead and multiple bruises and burns. But in this treatment facility, all their wounds are treated until they completely disappear. By the time they are released, their skin is picture perfect, like a baby. They are paraded in front of the cameras as if they were never hurt at all. They are made perfect, as if nothing had happened.

Although they are perfect on the outside, however, they both bear inner scars that have changed them for life. They have been marked forever by the horror that they endured and, by making them look perfect, the government has denied their suffering. This false perfection is almost worse than the games themselves.

We all know that when we see pictures of celebrities in glossy magazines, we are not seeing what they really look like. The photos are altered, all blemishes covered over by impressive computer technology. Thanks to Photoshop, stars can be made to look perfect: no wrinkles, no cellulite, no pock marks. They are flawless. And this is how we all want to look, right?

When Jesus appeared in the resurrected form, he came to us with scars. I find that strange, don't you? He showed us his wounds. If God could raise a person from death to life, surely God could have fixed all those messy wounds. So it must have been intentional that Jesus returns to us with scars. Why? When Jesus appears, he is recognized by his wounds. It is not his face that the disciples look at, or his voice that they hear. They know him by his scars.

We Americans find perfection beautiful. To be without blemish, without wrinkle or scar, this is our ideal. But for God, it is precisely our imperfections that make us beautiful. Our wounds mark our greatest lessons in life. Jesus came back with scars, and he was beautiful.

DAY 33 The Ripple Effect

I know your works. Look, I have set before you an open door, which no one is able to shut. (Revelation 3:8)

When my son Max was about two, we went for a walk. I pushed him in the stroller around a beautiful duck pond near our house in Kansas. We planned on feeding the ducks with some bread from the pantry. It was a beautiful Saturday morning and the sun was out. As is usual in Kansas, there was also a nice breeze.

We came to the duck pond and one of the ducks was swimming near the shore. Max got out of the stroller and started throwing pieces of bread into the water. The duck moved closer and began to eat. More ducks saw the action and began to move toward this new source of food.

Then Max saw a plastic wrapper on the ground right near the water. "Mom! Trash!" he yelled. We had talked before about how you don't throw trash on the ground.

"Yes, Max, let me pick that up so the ducks don't try to eat it."

"Yeah! So the ducks don't eat it!" he agreed.

We fed the ducks and began to walk around the pond. But now that Max had seen one piece of trash, he saw more.

A bottle. "Mom! Trash!!"

A can. "Mom! Trash!!"

A McDonalds bag. A cigarette box. A plastic bag. A beer bottle. A container.

I was picking up and picking up and picking up. I had to

put the trash in the only plastic bag I'd brought, and soon it was full. I was so glad Max wanted to do a good thing that I kept on picking up and picking up, but soon the bottom of the stroller was full.

Why had I never noticed how much garbage was cluttering our neighborhood? I thought we lived in a well-tended area, but all of a sudden, it seemed more like a dump. I started getting mad. How could people be so careless? With my anger came exhaustion and resentment. I realized that I was no longer enjoying myself, no longer happy to be outside. I just wanted to go home. But I felt trapped. I did not want Max to see me giving up.

When we got home, we both had to take a bath. I had to clean the stroller with bleach and I was in a bad mood.

Trying to do good is hard. Once you begin to serve God and to help people, it seems like all the world's problems become visible to you. You give one person some money and five more come asking for the same. You make a donation to a charity and start getting solicitations at home, and e-mails and publications. Your mailboxes are full of junk just because you sent ten bucks to some good cause. I start feeling like I'm drowning in requests. I get mad and resentful. These people don't care about me. They care about my money!

I give blood when the blood mobile comes to our church. I have O positive blood, the universal blood type. So the local blood bank has taken to leaving me messages at home. I give blood one month and within weeks, they are asking for more. Sometimes I worry they will bleed me dry.

Most practicing Christians understand that we are called by God to give. Jesus was very clear about this. But we must remember that when Jesus gave, he had a plan. Jesus gave his life away. He healed people, taught people, and cast out demons. But he also knew when to walk away, say no, and take time to be alone. Jesus had a strategic plan. He knew exactly what God had called him to do and he did it, no more and no less. He was focused on *his job*, the job that God gave him, and he stuck to the plan.

Jesus taught and healed the sick and entire villages sought him out. Women with stomach pain, children with fevers, men who could not walk—he healed them all. When darkness came, he fell asleep, probably exhausted.

But before the sun came up, often Jesus would get up and go away, alone, to a quiet place to pray. There, in the presence of God, he would reconnect with why God brought him to earth and what he was supposed to do.

After his prayer time, Jesus moved on, even though there were still people who were ill, still people who were hungry for his teaching. Everywhere, he encountered a woman hoping to become well, a sick child, an elderly man. These were real people with valid needs who were searching for Jesus and yet he continued to move. Jesus knew that God wanted him to make an initial impression in these villages and then move. He left without answering all their questions or solving all their problems, for he knew that God had a plan and it was his job to follow that plan. He didn't deviate from it.

Had Jesus stayed in one village and fixed every problem there, cured every illness, tended to every need, had he done what the people wanted, he might never have died on the cross for us. We would not have known him.

God's plan is always the best plan. You see, when you follow God's plan, you experience what I like to call the ripple effect. If you do what God has in mind for you and only what God has in mind for you, it is like a pebble hitting the water. Every problem may not be solved, but the ripples will impact and influence people in ways that you cannot imagine.

After I had served in Kansas for seven years, I began to believe that God was calling me to serve somewhere larger. Our church in Kansas was full on Sunday mornings. The congregation was healthy. I felt God urging me to begin to look elsewhere. But I didn't want to go. I loved those people.

But I believed that God had something new in mind for me. When my family and I were called to St. John's Cathedral in Jacksonville, to the very cathedral where I had preached my first sermon as a seminarian, I could not believe it.

Accepting this call from God had an unexpected ripple effect, in a way that had nothing to do with my ministry, in a way that had nothing to do with me at all.

The day we moved into our home in Jacksonville, a woman in her seventies who lived next door came to the front door with her grandson to welcome us to the neighborhood. Her grandson was exactly my son Max's age. The woman told me that her daughter, her grandson's mother, had been battling cancer since he was born. So the little boy spent a lot of time at his grandparents' house. He could not have brothers or sisters.

When she had seen that the house next door was for rent, the woman told me she had prayed to God. "Please," she said. "Please bring a five-year-old boy to live next door." And who should move in but Max? Those two boys have become best friends, probably for life. I had thought our move was all about me. But God was calling Max as well.

As you prepare to serve God, ground yourself in prayer. Worship regularly and find yourself a small group for support. Then ask God for guidance. Don't just give to everyone who asks without prayer and planning. Ask God for your focus, your personal vocation, and then stick to the plan. Don't let the results of your efforts or the overwhelming needs of the world deter you from what you and God have in mind. And check in with God daily to stay on track.

Find your focus, your particular role in the world, and God will bless you with the ripple effect. Your small acts of service will do more than you can imagine.

A wise woman once said something beautiful to me. She said that when Jesus hung on the cross and said, "It is finished," it was not that all the problems of the world had been solved. He said, "It is finished," because the job that God had given him was over. He had done the tasks that God had given him to do. His job was done. The Holy Spirit would take care of the rest and the ripples of Jesus' life would change the face of the earth.

It is not your job to save the world. That is God's job. All that you can do is seek to find what God asks of you and do that. That's all that God asks.

Your True Identity

[He] causes all, both small and great, both rich and poor, both free and slave, to be marked on the right hand or the forehead. (Revelation 13:16)

Peter was getting a divorce. He and his wife agreed to share custody of their two daughters, ages four and six. Peter, a successful banker, would pay child support.

A few months after the divorce was final, Peter's ex-wife began to refuse to let the girls stay with him. She began telling her therapist that Peter was sexually abusing his daughters. Peter's ex-wife filed for full custody on the grounds that her daughters were being abused.

Peter lived in a small town. His ex-wife seemed to be spreading the news everywhere. People began to look at him with suspicion. He lost friends. He felt that he had gone crazy. He had never inappropriately touched his daughters. After a lengthy legal battle, he was eventually exonerated and maintained custody of his girls, but in the eyes of many, suspicions lingered.

Peter's ex-wife gave him a false identity. He went from being considered trustworthy and respectable to being seen as an abuser of his own children. How could his life be turned upside down so quickly?

Baptism is about identity that can never be taken away. It is about who you are at your core, a child of God. John of Patmos had a vision in which he saw the baptized marked as Christ's own forever. They fully belong to God.

I love C.S. Lewis's *Chronicles of Narnia*. My favorite scene in *The Voyage of the Dawn Treader* involves the most difficult character in the book, Eustace Scrubb. Isn't that a perfect name for an absolute brat? And he was a brat: spoiled, self-centered, a know-it-all. Eustace thought the world of himself and worked only to cause others annoyance and even pain for laughs. His cousins drag him into Narnia on a ship called the Dawn Treader, where he does nothing but complain and get in the way. Not once does he offer to help the crew. He drinks and eats more than his fair share of the food.

The crew lands on an abandoned island and as they begin to work to replenish their supplies, Eustace characteristically wanders off to rest. He encounters a cave full of treasure. Greedily, he stuffs his pockets and falls asleep. Well, this is a magic land and when Eustace wakes up, he has changed into a dragon. He goes back to the ship and spends much time trying to communicate to the crew and to his cousins that he is, in fact, Eustace. Finally, he writes his identity in large letters in the sand.

The crew cannot sail away with a heavy dragon. Eustace begins to realize what a nuisance he has been. He begins to see himself through the eyes of others. He is mortified by the pain and annoyance he has created. He begins to help with the work and, now that he is a dragon, he can do the work of ten men. After weeks of work and struggle, he wanders off alone and finds Aslan the lion, the Christ figure. My favorite scene in the book takes place when Eustace suddenly has the urge to peel off his skin, to rid himself of his dragonness. He tries to scratch it off but finds layers and layers of dragon hide underneath. He tries again and again, while the lion watches. Then the lion speaks.

"You cannot do that alone," he says.

So Eustace, for the first time in his life, asks for help.

The lion uses his claws to tear a hole in the dragon, a wound that goes right to his heart. With force, Aslan pulls off a huge, scaly mess. It hurts. Eustace wonders if he will survive, but he wants so much to be free that he does not ask the lion to stop. Underneath it all, Eustace is naked and vulnerable. He feels raw. Aslan lifts the boy with his soft, padded paws and throws him into the water of a pool, where the boy smarts and then swims deliciously, realizing that he is a boy again.

Needless to say, Eustace is changed from that point on. He becomes the person he really was, at his core, all along. He becomes good. His identity is changed. Or, I should say, it is restored.

Who are you, really? You are made of layers of self-identification. Who are you?

Your desires? Your ambition? Your worries? Your feelings? Your relationships? Are you your job? Your marriage? Your skills? Your wealth? Your house?

Do you secretly call yourself "loser" or "wimp" or "fat" or "lost" or "dead?"

Think how many times we were asked as children, "Who are you going to be when you grow up?" When do we ever have an adequate answer to that question?

At your core, you truly have only one identity. You are a child of God, baptized into the body of Christ. You are called to serve Christ in a world that is driven by other forces. You are a resident alien, living in enemy territory. You belong to the king. Everything that you do, you must do for the king. Anything else will lead you astray.

Baptism is radical. It is a once-in-a-lifetime event. It is

a sign of something invisible that changes our entire lives, identifies our core purpose, makes us belong to something far greater than just ourselves.

Three things happen in this sacred act. You are *named*. You are *washed*. And you are *marked*.

God claims the deepest core of your being. Of course, as your life progresses, layers of false self will grow and emerge and sometimes you may feel that you are your job or your relationship. You may get lured into wanting to prove that you deserve respect or wealth. But deep down inside, God has already claimed you and nothing can take that away from you. Quietly, God has been calling you from the moment of your baptism.

You have already been marked for heaven. There is a place there for you. All you have to do is agree to go.

Day 35 The Feast

And the angel said to me, "Write this: Blessed are those who are invited to the marriage supper of the Lamb." (Revelation 19:9)

I find it fascinating that we did not fall from God's grace in Eden by committing murder or having illicit sex or anything so dramatic and interesting. We fell from Eden by eating.

Eve took fruit that the serpent offered her and she ate it and then she gave it to Adam and he ate it. They ate something. And from that day forward, human beings have felt naked and alone and separated from God.

It is no wonder that the book of Revelation tells us that there is a feast in heaven. God feeds us. God offers us what we were not given before. He gives us unlimited permission to eat. After being exiled from Eden, we are invited back inside.

But there is one major problem with this vision of heaven. We no longer have any idea what it really means to feast.

Most Americans have so much food at our fingertips that when we think of a feast, we think of calories and a feeling of being overstuffed. We think of chocolate cake that tastes so good and makes us feel guilty afterward. We think of drinking too much. We think of indulgence, cellulite, and hangovers.

I struggle with eating. I eat when I am bored or angry or tired or just feeling sorry for myself. I really should lose ten pounds but (especially when evening comes) I find myself putting food in my mouth, and not because I am hungry.

Why do we crave food we do not need? Why do we eat foods that taste good but are not good for our bodies? What does it mean to feast today?

In the time of Jesus, few people worried about being overweight, or not getting enough exercise. They worried about getting enough to eat each day to survive. Getting your daily bread was a real challenge for almost everyone. So the idea of an abundance of food was seen as heaven itself.

Scripture tells us, "Blessed are those who are invited to the marriage supper of the Lamb" (Revelation 19:9).

Perhaps we Americans should add a clause: "and, by the way, there are no calories in heaven."

Maybe then we could picture the joy of being fed, without self-consciousness or guilt or even fear. We could open our hearts as we open our mouths and simply let God feed us once more.

Week 6

James and Thomas

**Appearing
to James**

*Then he appeared to James, then to all the
apostles. (1 Corinthians 15:7)*

I can only imagine the scene, a family reunion like no
other. Jesus has come to his younger brother to reveal himself
as the son of God. James must have been shocked. Was this
really his brother, risen from the dead? And how had he
misunderstood Jesus' ministry for so long?

Strange how we cannot see clearly those we love. Our
family members are often the people we hurt the most. We
make up our minds about who they are far before God is
done with them. We say that we listen to them, but in reality
we hold on to a terribly constrained, limiting view of them.
We imprison them as we claim to know them.

Each of us is a mystery. Those who seem incapable of
change can at times turn their lives around, while others who
enjoy every opportunity stagnate and wallow in self-pity.
Each person we see possesses qualities of infinite goodness.
And yet we often can see no further than our own definition
of who we think they are.

Not long ago, my husband was talking to me about a
project at his office. I was nodding, when he turned to me
and said, "You don't listen to me anymore!"

I was taken aback. I had not interrupted him. I thought
I was paying attention. But I realized I couldn't recount
everything he had said. He was right. I wasn't listening.

How many times have I neglected to see the wonder of

this person I love, standing right beside me? His familiarity may be the greatest obstacle to my listening. In thinking that I know him, I stop paying attention.

When James saw his brother alive, he must have realized the gravity of his past mistakes. This was a brother who had tried to stop Jesus from teaching. He had tried to silence Jesus. He did these things out of self-preservation and embarrassment. He did not believe in his brother because to do so would have disrupted his comfortable world. But now, in one visit, his whole world was blown apart.

I have always imagined that he said he was sorry. So sorry. That he had no idea. And I imagine that Jesus, his brother who was God, smiled.

The Younger Brother

"I did not see any other apostle except James the Lord's brother." (Galatians 1:9)

James was Jesus' younger brother.

I have a younger brother. I also have three sons. I know how a younger brother, if healthy and outgoing, usually bothers his older siblings. The younger brother is set to outdo the older. Inevitable competition, some healthy, some not, ensues.

Jesus lived with his family for many years. We do not know exactly how long, but we know he went home with his parents at age eleven after being found talking with the rabbis in the temple in Jerusalem. We can assume that he lived in Nazareth for at least a few years with his parents and brothers before we hear of him again at his baptism in the Jordan River.

James, along with his other siblings and his mother, came to Jesus after Jesus' ministry had officially begun. Jesus' family came not to listen to his teachings but to make him come home. A crowd had gathered. James and his family declared that Jesus was "out of his mind" (Mark 3:21) and they tried to grab him. They were prepared to bring him home by force. They were certain Jesus was crazy, that he was not himself. Jesus' behavior was an embarrassment to them, so much so that they were openly hostile.

They just wanted life to go back to normal. They just wanted their brother back.

James did not believe in the divinity of Jesus while Jesus was alive. But Jesus appeared to James. Why? Because although James did not believe in him and had tried to stop his ministry, James did love him. Love was the determining factor in the resurrection appearances, not belief. In the case of James, it was the love of one brother for another.

When someone dies, their relatives will often ask me, "Will I see my loved one again?" The answer is a simple yes. Somehow the resurrected life binds together those who love one another. This much is clear. When Jesus instructs us to love our neighbors as ourselves, he is talking about us binding our souls to one another in a life beyond death. He is talking about salvation itself.

The Message within You

Therefore rid yourselves of all sordidness and rank growth of wickedness and welcome with meekness the implanted word that has the power to save your souls. (James 1:21–24)

At your baptism, you became an eternal being. Eternal life was planted within you like a seed in rich soil. The message, as James writes, is planted within you. All you have to do is welcome that message and let it grow, branching out to express itself in every aspect of your life.

An old Jewish folktale describes how each baby is knit together by God in the womb and within that sacred space of warmth and protection, the child possesses all knowledge and all wisdom. But just as the baby is being born, an angel of God descends and whispers a mysterious word in the child's ear. With the sound of that word, the child's knowledge of the universe is covered over, as we would cover an outdoor plant with a blanket on a cold evening in winter. And so the child comes into the world knowing nothing.

Maybe this explains how, when you are studying or learning a new concept, you may experience an "aha" moment when knowledge seems to click into place, like pieces of a puzzle. The problem to be solved resolves itself, and you feel like you had the answer all along. It feels as if you have simply uncovered something you had always known deep in the recesses of your being.

I took a physics class in college. It was physics for

nonmathematicians like me, but I still found myself lost in class. Often, I would approach the professor after class and simply say, "I don't get it!"

With patience and kindness, this good man would painstakingly explain the material over again for me. And sometimes, I would receive a burst of insight. It would come to me like a gift, a flash, a breath of fresh air. All of a sudden, what had confounded me made sense.

A mathematician once told me that he will often go to bed with a problem unsolved, a lingering mess in his mind. And at some point in the night, he will awaken to the knowledge of how to solve it. The answer just bubbles up into his subconscious like a gift.

The message is implanted within you. You do know what is best for you and you do know, deep down inside, what God is calling you to do. Be careful not to spend your life asking others for advice when the truth itself is within you, waiting to be uncovered. Trust in God to reveal your purpose, to uncover the wisdom that lives within you. You are wise. After all, you are a baptized child of the Most High.

Thomas and the Pull of God

Thomas said to him, "Lord, we do not know where you are going; how can we know the way?" (John 14:5)

When my friend Tom was growing up in Virginia, he loved to go down to the pond behind his house and just mess around, daydreaming. His parents were constantly scolding him for going off alone. But he loved the outdoors.

One winter when Tom was about six, he awoke on a Saturday and there was frost on the ground, not a normal occurrence in the South. His mother told him that he was not allowed to go to the pond. "It might be dangerous," she said. Tom ate breakfast and horsed around with his brother until about eleven o'clock, and then, though his brother was content to read, Tom got bored.

Tom snuck out of the house. He was excited by the glittering beauty of the frost and the icicles hanging from the trees. It was a glorious day. "I wonder if there is ice on the pond," he thought. And if he found ice, would it be strong enough to walk on?

When he reached the pond, he was pleased to see ice, lots of it. He put his foot on it and pressed down. Nothing happened. The ice appeared thick and strong. Tom stood on it, figuring that if the ice broke, he would only get his sneakers wet in the shallow water. Then he shuffled a bit further out. The ice seemed to hold. It was incredibly beautiful. "What if I cut a hole in the ice and tried to fish?" Tom got excited about this idea. He picked up a big rock.

Moving out onto the ice, carrying the rock, Tom eased his way to the center of the pond. He knew if he fell in now he would surely get soaked. He knew that he shouldn't be doing this, but the thrill was so great. This was just like a movie!

Just as he about to throw the stone on the ice to make a fishing hole, he heard a voice. It was a long way off, but he heard it distinctly.

"Hmm!!" It sounded a bit like his mother. He couldn't make out her word, but it sounded like his name. Was she calling for him? She would be furious if she knew that he had come down to the pond. Maybe he was hearing things.

He waited. Nothing. Thank God, it was just his imagination. He got ready to throw the stone. "Tom!"

Oh, no, there it was again, the voice. It sounded much more familiar and it was louder, closer. Could he pretend that he didn't hear?

"TOM!" It was definitely his mother. She didn't sound happy. He inched his way off the pond with the stone, going the other way so that he could hide from her in the woods. He thought if he could run and hide, he could get back to the house before she did and pretend he'd been there all the time.

"THOMAS WAYNE JOHNSON!!" Oh no. She'd used his full name. She was mad. He stood on the side of the shore of the pond, put down the stone, and waited for the worst to happen.

"THOMAS WAYNE JOHNSON, you come home this minute!!" Oh, well. The jig was up. He began to run back toward the voice, expecting certain punishment. He got to the house. His mother stood on the porch with her hands on her hips.

"Come inside," she said.

So inside he went, into the large kitchen. And there he saw all his friends from first grade, with a huge cake and presents. His dad, even his granddad and grandma were there. You see, he wasn't in trouble at all. He had forgotten it was his own birthday!

If we are really quiet, we can hear God's voice. I am talking about the call of God, a "pull" you might say. What is pulling on your heart? Where is the light in your life, the courage, the spark? Ask yourself these questions and something will urge you into the direction that Christ would walk. And then you will know that you have heard the voice of God.

Most of us in the church are trying to follow that call. But we spend a lot of time stalling and questioning, doubting and hiding. Like Tom, I think we believe that if we truly follow the pull, we will be punished. We hear a voice, which is sometimes stern, but always loving. And we get scared. We pretend that we don't hear.

Many people have said to me, "Oh, I don't hear voices!" Of course you don't, but when you are quiet and when you pray, can't you often identify the path that is most loving? Sometimes God calls us in many directions, but I believe that most people know what is best for them and what is most faithful to God in their daily lives. If you do identify that for yourself, what are you waiting for? You don't have to hear an audible voice or touch physical wounds to know that God is calling you.

Why do we run when we feel the pull to move closer to God? Why do we pretend we don't hear? Why do we inch away? I think we expect God to make us suffer for our faults. We find ourselves unworthy and we are scared of losing our comfort. Repenting, following God's call, may feel like work. It may feel like a drag, a burden. And it may be scary, because we have to give up control. But this actually brings freedom and joy. It releases us from the past, and gives us new life.

Think of Tom, having fun on the ice, then afraid that he'd get in trouble, ignoring the call. Even running away. And almost missing the great party.

There is a folktale about a man who gets to heaven to find St Peter standing at the gate. St Peter asks him his name and occupation. "John Fowler" the man says. "Engineer."

"Oh, yes, welcome home, John!" St. Peter opens the gate and invites John into heaven.

"Wait!" John says. "That's it? You're just going to let me in? What about the time that I lied and almost cheated on my wife?"

"Yes, John, this is the way it works."

John could see streets of gold inside, more beautiful than anything he had seen before, and he backed up a step. "No, this isn't right. I am not ready. You don't mean me."

"Oh, yes we do, John. We mean you."

"No, that is too bright. I have too many faults. God must not be aware of my faults."

"Oh, but he is, John and he welcomes you inside."

With each word, John took another step back until finally

he said, "I just can't do this." And he turned around and walked away from heaven.

Thomas asked Jesus, "How can we know the way?"

I want to suggest to you that you do know the way. Most of us, deep down inside, know right from wrong and what God would have us do. What we lack is the strength and courage to actually follow, because the way is unfamiliar and when we are awed by the brightness, we would rather argue within ourselves about whether we can actually hear God. Or feel the pull. Trust that you do hear the voice of the risen Christ. Trust that you have known all your life about God's love for you and God's will for you. And begin to move in the direction of that voice.

The Easter joy awaits us all who have the courage to give in to the pull of God. But sometimes we pretend that we don't hear and we spend our lives waiting on the periphery of joy, taking a step back whenever we are invited to move inside. Which will it be for you?

The Ascension

As they were watching, he was lifted up. (Acts 1:9)

When I graduated from college, I found myself battling sadness that I did not understand. Like many young people, I struggled with who I was, and what my future held.

It was then that I was blessed to find a wonderful therapist who listened to me intently. He was gentle and kind.

For the first three months of our sessions, all I did was cry. I don't remember at all what I talked about, but I remember being stunned by the volume of tears that flowed. And I was stunned that he didn't tire of me. He never yawned or kicked me out of his office.

One aspect of our therapy made me mad. Every session, when fifty minutes were up, he would look at me and say, with a smile, "Time's up!"

It did not matter if I was right in the middle of a cosmic insight or if I was crying frantically. Time was up. It was time for me to leave.

Part of me wanted to yell at him. "CAN'T I JUST HAVE FIVE MORE MINUTES?" What was all the rush? Why did our time have to end so abruptly?

Then, one day, I read about the Ascension. Jesus also said, "Time's Up!" He left the disciples, physically and clearly, without any room for them to doubt. "It's up to you now," he was saying. "Our time is up."

I realized that part of the reason that my time in that therapist's office was so sacred, so valuable to me, was because it was limited. I valued every moment of that time because

I knew that it would not last forever. That made it more precious.

After the resurrection, on the fortieth day, Jesus was lifted up into heaven. The disciples were left standing below, not knowing what to do next. They felt lost and probably a little mad. How dare he leave? They still needed him! How could he abandon them like that?

But now we can see that they would have never become leaders in the early church if Jesus had stuck around. He had to leave so that they could begin to reflect and appreciate the time that they had with him. When he left, they actually became more like him.

DAY 41 Shalom

*When it was evening on that day, the first day
of the week, and the doors of the house . . . were
locked for fear of the Jews, Jesus came and stood
among them and said, "Peace be with you." (John
20:19)*

When I look out at my parishioners on Sunday, I can see
their fear. I see the face of a teenage girl whose parents are
divorcing, the elderly woman who will not get a colonoscopy
even though her mother died of colon cancer, the man who
does not know how to clean or do laundry since his wife
died. I see the parents who struggle with a child who has
ADHD and the lonely middle-aged woman who is too
frightened to try to meet someone.

All of them are afraid. Their fears are unique, but they
are all afraid, and so am I. If we are honest with ourselves,
we all are afraid. Deep down inside, we realize that our lives
are out of our control. We do not know what will happen
tomorrow and the unknown is scary.

When Jesus appears to Thomas and the disciples, his first
words are, "Peace be with you. Shalom."

Before he was crucified, we know that Jesus was afraid.
He asked God to take this cup from him. He did not want
the pain of the cross. But after the resurrection, he was no
longer afraid. Not only was Jesus at peace, but he offered his
peace to us.

If you chose to put your trust in the fact that there is life
after this life, then you have nothing to fear. Nothing. It is

hard to grasp, but once you are not afraid of dying, then there is nothing to fear in this world.

I do not think that many of us have any concept of true peace. For us, peace is just the absence of war, but the peace that the resurrected Christ conveys is a state of perfect harmony between a person and the universe. It is balance itself. It is joy.

When Jesus said, "Peace be with you," he was giving his followers a gift. We need never be afraid again.

DAY 42 Touching God

[Thomas] said to them, "Unless I see the marks of the nails in his hands, and put my finger in the mark of the nails and my hand in his side, I will not believe." (John 20:25)

I know many Thomases. I know many people with rational, scientific minds, people who cannot seem to swallow the resurrection. And why should they? It makes no logical sense that we should exist when our bodies lie in the ground. Or does it?

I used to argue with those who doubted the resurrection, but that does not work. The resurrection cannot be proven by scientific formula. It is an otherworldly event. But it can be experienced. That is how Jesus brought Thomas around.

When Jesus went to see his followers, he made a special visit to that upper room just for Thomas. Jesus knew that highly intellectual types need to touch him to believe.

In our scientific age, how do we touch Jesus today? It is not impossible. It can be done. Not physically, of course, but spiritually, we can still touch the risen Christ. So this is my advice to all you brilliant doubters out there.

If you want to believe in the resurrection, in God the Almighty and the event of the Incarnation, then you must touch it through practice.

When someone comes to my office who wants to believe and cannot, I ask them if they are willing to give six months to an experiment. Some of them are not willing to do this, but most are hungry to try. So I ask them to practice the faith.

"I know that you don't believe," I say, "but, for six months, I want you to act as if you do believe."

I ask them to attend church every Sunday and spend twenty minutes a day in prayer of some kind. I ask them to find a way to serve the poor and give of their money and resources. During those months, I pretty much leave them alone.

An old friend of mine once said that receiving Holy Communion is like letting water drip on a rock. It quietly and slowly forms you. If a person is willing to truly live in faith, to touch the story itself as Thomas reached out and touched the scars of Christ, he or she will often experience something that brings it all alive.

Sometimes, they simply find that when their six months are up, they do not want to stop. They feel that life without the practice, without touching the faith, is empty for them. And that can be enough. That is really enough.

Week 7

....

The Holy Spirit

DAY 43 The Unreasonable Spirit

When he had said this, he breathed on them and said to them, "Receive the Holy Spirit. If you forgive the sins of any, they are forgiven." (John 20:22–23)

Sometimes I think that Jesus is just plain unreasonable.

Love your enemies, he tells us. Pray for those who persecute you. When someone slaps you, turn and offer to let them slap your other cheek.

Love the IRS auditor? Love the guy who cuts you off on the highway? Love the bank teller who won't waive your overdraft fees? Love the health insurance executive who refuses to pay a claim? Love the bully who makes your child suffer at school?

I remember a young woman who came to me years ago to tell me that her uncle had raped her years before. I did not say that she was supposed to love him. How could I? All I could do was listen and assure her that God still loved her, even when she cut herself and wanted to die. All I could do was hear her pain. And when she finally expressed anger about the man who hurt her so badly, when she got mad, I was grateful. I felt like saying, "Yes! Get mad!"

When a victim appears depressed instead of angry, I really begin to worry. Isn't it right just to be angry at someone who hurts you?

Who is Jesus kidding? How in the WORLD can we love our enemies?

What about terrorists who fly planes into skyscrapers or set off bombs in subways? What about serial killers? Or pedophiles? What about them? What could it possibly mean to love them?

Jesus couldn't have meant what he said. Or could he?

Just when I think that he was asking too much, asking what no human being could possibly do, the image of Jesus hanging on the cross comes to me and I remember his words:

"Father, forgive them. They do not know what they are doing."

And I begin to believe, once more, that Jesus knew exactly what he was talking about when he told us to love our enemies. And God knows we can do it.

What was Jesus able to do on that cross that we cannot seem to do? How could he love so much and so unconditionally? It has to do with perspective. Jesus knew that we would not be able to follow his instructions without the gift of the Holy Spirit and one of the Holy Spirit's greatest gifts is perspective.

If you and I can believe in the resurrection without hesitation, if we can really trust that nothing will separate us from the love of God and that our souls are destined to live with Christ in a life far exceeding this one, then everything changes.

The reason that we hate or run away or want to seek vengeance is because we are afraid. We are afraid that the harm that has been done to us has ruined us. We are afraid that we will never be the same. But if you knew that *no one* could separate you from God's love, and that even if someone murdered you, you would be fine, better than fine, then everything would change.

You would stop worrying about yourself. And you could

begin to think of the soul of the other. You could begin to see your tormenter as human, even if all that appears before you is evil. You could see that some sliver of the light of Christ just might be dimly lit in even the worst human being. It might be. And you would honor that possibility.

Do you really believe that everything will be OK? Do you trust that God has a place for you, a life for you that is everything that you have ever wanted and more? Do you believe this?

If you do, then you can love your enemies. You can begin to see them for who they are and even risk your life for them. But if you do not trust in the resurrection of our Lord, then how can you be expected to love those who mistreat you?

And let me be clear that by love, I do not mean that you should like your persecutors or even have warm feelings for them. That is beyond your control. But when you are mistreated, you must treat the perpetrator with kindness, compassion, honesty. And you do this for God and the very salvation of your soul.

I woke up very early one morning and saw the moon shining on my face, full and beautiful. And I knew that it was shining on all of us, the homeless man waking up by a curb, the exhausted young mother, the abuser who beat his wife, the thief, and the murderer. That moon shined its light on all of us and in its light I was reminded that God invites all of us to the table. God wants all of us to come inside.

It is all about seeing things from the Spirit's perspective.

From the Spirit's perspective, we all fall short. We all need another chance again and again and again. From the Spirit's perspective, life is a brief training ground for the life eternal. From the Spirit's perspective, suffering gives us an opportunity to show forth the love and strength of Christ. And every time we love our enemies, God's light shines through us.

So when that guy cuts you off or the woman at the bank won't help you or when, God forbid, you get hurt or robbed or your children are bullied, remember that this moment is not the end of the story. Remember that through the power of the Holy Spirit, you have been invited to pray for, to forgive, and yes, even to love those who hurt you.

The Kingdom Dimension

Jesus taught them, "When you pray, say, 'Father, hallowed be your name. Your kingdom come.'"
(Luke 11:2)

When I was in high school, I signed up for a course on movement and drama. At the beginning of every class, the teacher would gather us in the gym and we would stretch. He told us to spread out on the floor so we had plenty of room. He always kept the fluorescent lights turned off. Every day, we could see a spot of sunlight out on the floor, where the early afternoon rays shone through a skylight to make a perfect bright circle. During every class, I wanted to plant myself right in that circle of light, but I always got shy and moved to a dimmer corner to do my warm-ups. I wondered what it would be like to dance in that brightness, but I was embarrassed to call attention to myself, so I shied away.

Jesus taught the disciples the Lord's Prayer. The greatest of all Christian prayers, the Lord's Prayer is profound. Its words have remained intact through the centuries. Whereas the Nicene Creed and other statements and prayers have been composed by clergy and committees, the Lord's Prayer slips like liquid through the theological disputes of the centuries and remains today a symbol of the beauty and majesty of God. Jesus himself spoke this prayer. It is simply too holy to mess with.

Contemplate this phrase:

Thy kingdom come.

Jesus told us to say to God, "Thy kingdom come." What was he trying to say?

In Jesus' day, a kingdom was an area of land governed by a monarch. It was a place where the laws were created and enforced by the king and no one else. There was one ruler to whom all others were subservient. Depending on the ruler, a kingdom could be either a glorious and good place or a bad and cruel place. The kingdom of God would be a place where God was in charge, where God made the rules for all of us to follow. Since God is inherently good, God's kingdom would be a land of peace and harmony beyond anything that humans could muster. Even our greatest prosperity and peace would be no match for God's kingdom, for the ruler of God's kingdom would institute justice and righteousness like we have never seen.

Today in most of the world, we have lost the notion of kingdom. When we think of rulers, we think of Queen Elizabeth, lovely and very wealthy, but in reality she is a figurehead with little political authority. Those lands that are governed today by absolute rulers tend to be places of violence, poverty, and great inequality between rich and poor. The only references we see to kingdoms today are found in fairy tales, or as part of the Disney empire.

No wonder the kingdom of God means little to us.

We often view the kingdom of God as heaven, the place we hope to go after we die, the reward after a good life of prayer and service. But this is a misunderstanding. We misunderstand resurrection itself if we think that it only exists after we die. Jesus clearly stated that the kingdom of God was near and he wanted us to pray for it to come not when we die but *now*, on earth as it is in heaven.

Jesus was talking about a realm of God that already exists but that people are not somehow able to access. It is like having the best computer game, but not downloading it. We are living in a half-life, not allowing the God dimension to illumine us. Without allowing the kingdom of God to come, we are only half alive.

Scientists are aware of three dimensions that we can see. The fourth dimension is considered to be time. And beyond time? Could there be dimensions that exist right now, right here, that are somehow beyond our perception?

In my high school drama class, there came a day when I took a chance. When the teacher asked us to spread out and begin to dance, I went to the sunlight. I stood there, in the middle of the circle of light and began to reach upward. The air itself was full of the tiny particles that you can only see when you are standing in direct sunlight. The light was so bright that it blinded me. I was not able to see anyone else around me so I couldn't compare myself to others or even contemplate embarrassment. I danced and it felt so beautiful. I caught a glimpse of the God dimension.

Once you have tasted the God dimension, the presence of God among us, you want that presence all the time and that is when you start praying in earnest:

Thy kingdom come.

Thy dimension come.

Not long ago, I had the privilege of visiting a parishioner in an assisted living facility. Barbara is a long-standing, faithful member of the cathedral who spent years serving in our altar guild. She is now bedridden. Our parishioners bring her communion regularly. She has the look of one who is living in the God dimension. Light shines from her eyes.

"Sometimes I get frustrated because I cannot walk, but then I realize that I need to follow God," she told me. "Whenever I have tried to live life my way, I have ended up making a mess. When I step out in front of Jesus, then I can't see him or follow him because I have put myself first. So I step back into his presence, letting him lead me so that I can see his light and follow his path for me. He presses upon me and guides me, not with words but with his patient presence."

God waits for you in the God dimension and you can access God there now. Simply step into the light, God's place, a resurrection life.

The Logos

*In the beginning was the Word, and the Word
was with God, and the Word was God. . . .
[The Word] was life and the life was the light of
all people. (John 1:1, 4)*

Helen Keller is buried at the National Cathedral in
Washington, DC. The famous scholar and writer became
deaf and blind after a terrible illness in early childhood. As a
result, she grew up savagelike in a home full of people who
did not understand her. As recounted in the play *The Miracle
Worker*, Helen is saved by a young woman who comes to
teach her. After months of battles, the young woman, Annie
Sullivan, teaches Helen to eat properly and behave. But Helen
remains alone in darkness. Over and over again, Annie spells
letters into Helen's hands. Helen mimics the spelling, but she
is never able to connect the letters with the meaning of a
word. The actual connection between a word and an object
eludes her.

One day, Helen feels her way to the water pump in her
family's yard. As Helen pumps the water and lets it run
cool over her hands, Annie spells the word "W-A-T-E-R."
Water. Again, Annie spells water into Helen's palm as the
cool liquid runs over her hand and out between her fingers.

Helen stops pumping. She would later write that in that
moment, she awoke to life. All had been darkness until
that moment. She had been completely and totally alone in
a world with no meaning. But in that one moment, Helen
recalled the one word that she had learned when she was just

a toddler, right before she became ill. The word, as she had pronounced it, was *WAWA*.

Helen realized that the word "wawa" was a way of connecting to the liquid that had poured over her hand. Life and light entered her mind and her world, literally, began that day. She was born to the Word and the Word was born in her.

God is the Word. God is the Connection. God is the *aha* moment.

God is present in the office of a therapist who has counseled and listened to the same patient for years. On a particular day, the therapist gently repeats an insight that he has had and is able to communicate to the man a pattern in his behavior so that the man can see, for the first time in his life, that he is wounded, that he is good, and that he is loved. God is present in a concert hall when someone plays music that lifts a soul to levels it has never experienced and a young woman in the audience weeps and cannot explain why.

This is the Logos, the Word, the connection. This is the Spirit of God

DAY 46 The Moment When an Apostle Is Made

He breathed on them and said to them, "Receive the Holy Spirit." (John 20:22)

It was early evening in Montgomery, Alabama, in December 1955. An African-American woman in her midforties boarded a bus. She carried herself in a dignified manner. You wouldn't have known from looking at her that she had been stooped over an ironing board all day. Her shoulders ached and her feet were swollen. She took a seat at the front of the bus.

As the bus moved through the city streets, it filled with passengers on their way home from work. After a few stops, the driver turned to look at the woman. He told her that she needed to move so that a white person could take her seat.

With one word, Rosa Parks changed the course of American history. Just one word, spoken quietly. She just said, "No."

When a policeman came to arrest her, she told him that this did not make sense, that it wasn't fair. He told her that he agreed, it wasn't fair, but it was the law.

Later that evening, thousands of people would gather at a Baptist church in a poor section of Montgomery. At that church, Dr. Martin Luther King would say, "There comes a time when people get tired of being trampled over by the iron feet of oppression."

There comes a time in the life of a person . . .

Two thousand years ago, one hundred and twenty people

came together in a room. They all had known and loved Jesus. He had appeared to them in joyful encounters after his resurrection, but now he had been lifted out of their sight. And they had no idea what to do next.

Peter addressed the group. "Jesus chose twelve of us but now there are only eleven. Judas Iscariot has left us for good. We must fill his seat at the table, so that there are twelve once more." The number twelve was sacred. There were twelve tribes of Israel. So there must be twelve to continue Jesus' work in the world.

Peter said, "We have discussed this matter and identified two men who could fill this seat. One is Joseph or Barsabas, sometimes called Justus, and the other is Matthias."

I can just picture Matthias, standing there in the middle of the crowd, thinking, "Who, me? What about that guy over there? I didn't know Jesus well enough. I am not ready. This could be a lot of work. Where is the door?"

In ancient Greek, the name "Matthias" means disciple. A disciple is literally one who learns. A disciple is an apprentice.

I believe that there are three basic stages in the life of a Christian. The first is baptism, when God opens the kingdom of God to us and our resurrection life begins. And though God welcomes us, we must spend a lifetime saying yes to that invitation.

The second stage is that of discipleship, when we realize that we want to devote time and energy to learn about Jesus, to try to be like him. We attend worship, we study and read. In discipleship, we may join a group of fellow believers, where we can honestly speak about our joys and sorrows.

Eventually, God will invite us to the third stage of the life of faith. This is the life of the apostle. The word "apostle" means one who is sent. The twelve were called disciples during Jesus' life on earth, but after his resurrection and ascension, they became known as apostles, because God said, "It's your turn. I need you to do my work in the world. Here is my Spirit as your guide. Get to work."

The invitation that the Spirit extends to become an apostle is different for each person, and often comes unexpectedly. Rosa Parks had no idea that she was about to start a civil rights movement. Matthias had no idea he would be invited to become an apostle. They were just being faithful in the moment. So we must study, pray, worship, give, and watch for the moments when God asks something of us, the moment when we are sent.

Ingrid was born and raised in Germany. At the age of twenty-three, she fell madly in love with an American graduate student. When he asked her to marry him, she was thrilled. They wed and moved to Cincinnati, Ohio.

She found herself living in a foreign country with a man she did not know well. Soon, she was pregnant with their first child and gave birth to a girl who was healthy but demanding. Ingrid felt both exhausted and alone.

As a baptized Christian, Ingrid knew enough to find a church, where people cuddled her baby and took an interest in her. She felt loved. Ingrid met an apostle at our church named Sarah. Every week, Sarah was sent by God to bring communion to people at a nursing home who were too frail to come to church.

At the nursing home, Sarah met an elderly widow who had recently lost her husband after fifty years of marriage. The old woman had stopped speaking. The staff was at a loss and asked Sarah to pray for her, and mentioned that the woman had immigrated to the U.S. from Germany with her family when she was in high school.

As Sarah was praying for this silent woman, Ingrid's face came to her mind. At church the next Sunday, she invited Ingird to come to the nursing home with her.

Ingrid had all the same thoughts as Matthias, "Who me? I am managing a baby! I am exhausted all the time! I am sad and lonely and someone needs to care for me! Where is the door?" But Ingrid did not speak all of these thoughts. She just agreed.

Ingrid met the old woman later that afternoon. In German, she introduced herself and told her how happy she was to meet her.

"Danke! Ich bin so glücklich!" said the woman, hugging her. "Thank you! I am so happy!" Suddenly the woman could not stop talking, laughing, and crying in her native German.

Ingrid ended up visiting the woman often. They became good friends. The old woman found a reason to speak and a reason to live. And Ingrid learned how to be a good mother.

A moment will come for you too. A moment of the Spirit, in which you are called to become an apostle. Will you let yourself be sent?

DAY 47 The Glory of God

For he received honor and glory from God the Father when that voice was conveyed to him by the Majestic Glory. (2 Peter 1:17)

St. Mary's is a little mission church near downtown Jacksonville. The church serves those in poverty, the homeless, and the mentally ill. The Cathedral has quietly supported this parish for years.

One afternoon, one of our parishioners took me to a Bible study at St. Mary's. She parked the car when we arrived, and we saw a tiny boy sitting on the sidewalk crying his eyes out. He could not have been more than two years old. He had great clumps of braided hair that stuck out from every side of his little head. He wore a blue shirt and plaid shorts. His eyes were red and blotchy from crying so hard. A young woman who looked like she could be his mother stood nearby talking to some friends. She was holding a pink bundle, a newborn baby girl.

I went over to the little boy and knelt down to ask him if he was OK. He held out his arms for me to carry him. I picked him up and, man, did he hold on. He pressed his little self up against me and put his head on my shoulder. His crying stopped like a faucet had just been turned off. I held him and rocked him and felt so peaceful for a moment.

His mother came over, grabbed him around his waist, and pulled him from me. He started to scream again. "He always goes to strangers," she said to me abruptly. My heart sank. I had to walk away with him crying again, knowing that the moment of peace that we had together only made him long for more.

Sometimes there is so much pain in the world that I do not know what to do. I cried for that little boy later that day, just like I cried for the children in Russia that I knew years ago when I worked in orphanages there. I remember a little baby girl who cried so hard. She had been found in a dumpster just days before I met her and when she cried, I imagined she was desperate for her mother to come for her. She had the most beautiful blue eyes.

When I encounter children who need more that I can give them, I wonder how God can cope with so much pain. If it hurts my heart, God's heart must be broken.

The word "glory" means brightness. Glory is the part of God that we cannot even bear to look at, the *doxa,* a word used only for God and God alone. Only God is bright, and the paradox is this: God is most glorified in the midst of pain and suffering. The Son of God could only be made bright through the shame and suffering he endured. The brightness of God shines forth in the hardest of places and the darkest of times. The greater the darkness, the more the *doxa* of God stands out and shines.

Resurrection is born out of the pit of death and despair. Moments of pain, moments of darkness and abandonment are the greatest moments to glorify God.

The light shines in the darkness and the darkness shall not overcome it. The light shines in the darkness.

God is best glorified in the places of hopelessness and despair. God is glorified in the heart of our cities whenever we find a job for someone who needs one, whenever we hold a child who is crying. Whenever we help find shelter for a family who needs a roof over their heads, God is glorified.

When my youngest son Max was little, we used to have great conversations on the way to and from preschool. One morning he asked me, "Mom, if you were a superhero, who would you be?"

I thought about it for a moment and I came up with Water Woman. I could swim to the bottom of the deepest oceans and plant my feet on the ground, then jump and touch the moon, only to come back into the water again. And I could understand the songs of the whales.

Sometimes, I really wish I could be Water Woman—or at least someone a lot more powerful than Kate Moorehead. I wish I could take that little boy that I held outside St. Mary's and make his life better. I want to be able help every child I see who is in despair. I feel powerless.

But I can use these moments of helplessness to glorify God. I can let my prayers rise to touch the moon and God will be glorified. Each time we welcome the stranger, God is glorified. Each time we bring hope to the despairing, comfort to the dying, volunteer at a youth center, bring good news to the hopeless, God is glorified.

Deacon Ben Clance goes out of our cathedral each week into a maximum security prison. There, in the midst of darkness and despair, he glorifies God by bringing communion to the inmates. When a prisoner is about to be executed, Ben washes his feet, giving him the chance to turn his heart to God even at the last.

Ben can't undo the crimes these prisoners have committed. He can't free them from their jail cells. But he brings God's light to them.

It is not your job to fix the world. That is God's work. But it is your job and my job to go into the places of darkness and despair and let God's light shine. We are called to glorify God, one moment at a time. Let God work in you. Become His hands and feet. Work one small miracle at a time. Let God be glorified in you.

DAY 48 Spirit Evangelism

Go therefore and make disciples of all nations.
(Matthew 28:19)

My parents were searching for God when I was born. They studied many of the world's religions. When I was six months old, they decided to become Hindu.

The branch of Hinduism that they practiced is called Vedanta, founded by the Hindu teacher and saint Ramakrishna. Basically, Ramakrishna practiced all of the world's major religions and concluded that they were all valid paths to God. He found God in Christianity, in Judaism, in Buddhism, and in Islam, as well as his own native Hinduism.

I remember traveling to an ashram in New York City to visit the swami with my parents. They tell the story that, when I was two years old, I tried to climb up on the swami's head. The swami said it was a sign that I was an old soul. My parents sang bhajans, Hindu songs about God. They dedicated a room in our house as a chapel. We would burn incense and sing to Ramakrishna and his wife, Holy Mother.

My parents' foray into Hinduism was not ultimately fulfilling and, in the end, the swami advised them to return to the religion of their culture, to Christianity. He taught them that the deepest impressions of their childhoods came from Christianity and hence their hearts would be most open to God in this tradition.

So at the age of five, I was baptized into the Episcopal Church. The memory is vivid to me. I remember how the minister poured water on my forehead and *marked me as*

Christ's own forever. I consider my baptism to be the most important moment of my life.

I grew up running and playing in church while my mother practiced the organ. I would take off my shoes and run and slide down the aisles in my socks. I love Jesus and now I am an Episcopal priest. And I ponder and sometimes struggle with my relationship to the faithful of other religions.

Why did God raise me up in such a unique household? What am I to make of my Hindu roots? When I became a devout Christian, I ignored those roots. I felt that they were something strange and quirky, something to be hidden, a dark part of my past. But it was by God's providence that I encountered such richness and diversity at a young age. It has given me a unique understanding of what it means to be a Christian evangelist in a global world.

Evangelism, the spreading of the gospel, has been only partially understood for centuries. For hundreds of years Christians associated conversion with battle. To win people to Christianity involved conquering them, defeating them.

But sharing God's love means helping people celebrate their authentic selves. Evangelism is driven by the Holy Spirit. It is all about love.

Think of how a child reacts when she hears music. Her knees begin to move, then her legs, her arms, her hands. Soon every inch of her small body is dancing without embarrassment or fear. She is too young to have learned to be intimidated or afraid. She is free to dance. She responds without fear to the movement of the Holy Spirit.

What can you do to liberate yourself to dance with the spirit of God? God has unique and wonderful vocations for each of us. Each one of us is called to glorify God in a special way, a way that only the Holy Spirit can reveal to us. But we cannot move into our vocation if we are afraid. Fear paralyzes us. It stops the dancing.

"Do not be afraid," the angel said.

Do not be afraid of who you are. You are powerful, beautiful, and holy in God's eyes. You are a child of God.

Wisdom and the Parking Space

But the hour is coming, and is now here, when the true worshippers will worship the Father in spirit and truth, for the Father seeks such as these to worship him. (John 4:23)

The church where I served in Kansas was on the main thoroughfare through the city. Next to us, on the same side of the road, was a Roman Catholic Church. Our parking lots were divided only by a small side street.

It did not take me long after I arrived to realize that there was a war going on between the Roman Catholics and the Episcopalians over spaces in our parking lots. On Sunday mornings our parishioners would snap at Catholics they caught parking in our lot and the Catholics would glare if an Episcopalian took up a space in their lot.

The Catholics started talking about putting pictures of the pope on Episcopalians' cars in their lot. Our folks talked about putting *Episcopal Church Welcomes You* bumper stickers on cars in our lot belonging to Catholics.

Finally the Roman Catholic priest and I met, exasperated by our parishioners. We talked about posting signs that said "Jesus said 'Love thy neighbor.' So share thy parking spaces, for God's sake."

We are so concerned about reserving a spot for ourselves in life. We think, what is my role? Do people like and respect me? What is my place in society, in my career, in my family?

In our church parking lot feud, people from both churches

obsessed about the past (did you see who dared to take up space in our parking lot last week?) and about the future (what if people from that other church take all our spaces next Sunday?). This caused nothing but division and discord.

The Holy Spirit asks us to be aware of life beyond this life, to be awake. You cannot become wise by obsessing about the past or trying to predict the future. The wise men who found the baby Jesus were wise because they were paying attention. They were aware, awake in the present moment. And they were willing to leave behind their parking spaces and follow the light of a star.

We really have two options in life. We can focus on where we are parked and where we will park, or we can let go and move out into the unknown darkness of the present moment. Remember that God does not move in the past or in the future. God's name is not "I WAS" or "I WILL BE." It is "I AM." So to see God, to find God, you must be present in this very moment and you cannot hold on to anything. To find God means to be truly awake.

One of our parishioners has a rare brain disease. The doctors predicted he would live for about six months and we have prayed for a miracle. As I write this, he continues to defy the expectations of the doctors.

During his treatment, another miracle has happened to this man. He has become wise. He lives in the present moment. He cherishes every single thing: the beautiful sky outside his house, his granddaughter's artwork, his music. He is alive and present more than ever before, despite his illness.

We don't know what God will do or how long we will have this man with us, but we do know one thing. Our friend is awake. He is teaching us how to live. And what does he love to do most? He loves to come to church with a cross around his neck and talk to people about God.

There is an old folktale about awareness. A man is running from a tiger. The tiger chases him and the man runs off a precipice. As he is falling, the man grabs the roots of a tree protruding from the earth. He holds on for dear life and looks up to see the tiger pacing and growling above him. He looks down to see a cobra slithering and hissing in the grass below. He looks at the tree roots and notices that a small mouse is nibbling at the roots. And right above him, hanging on a branch, is a honeycomb. The honey drips quietly onto the back of his hand. The man licks the honey and it is so sweet.

That is the story of our lives. Our past is the tiger, who hunts us down and paces around, hoping to seize our minds and devour us with all the mistakes we've made or with voracious longing for the way things were. The future is the cobra, who slithers around waiting to wrap us in fears and hopes and plans for tomorrow. Even the present moment is nibbled away by the mouse. But in this very *now*, the sweetness of God is available for us to savor, a free gift, sweet and rare and beautiful. It is up to us to taste it.

Do you want to be wise? Do you want to find God? Then wake up. Be aware. The Spirit speaks not in the past or in the future but in the present moment. This very moment is where eternity meets reality. This is resurrection.

The Pentecost

> *When the day of Pentecost had come, they were all*
> *together in one place. And suddenly from heaven*
> *there came a sound like the rush of a violent*
> *wind, and it filled the entire house where they*
> *were sitting. Divided tongues, as of fire, appeared*
> *among them, and a tongue rested on each of them.*
> *All of them were filled with the Holy Spirit and*
> *began to speak in other languages, as the Spirit*
> *gave them ability. (Acts 2:1–4)*

Wayne was very sick with cancer throughout his old body. His wife lay beside him day and night, holding him. I would come to their house and pray with them. We knew he was dying. He slipped into a coma. For almost two weeks, he did not speak or eat.

Then one morning, he sat straight up in his bed and shouted, "Jean! I'm going!! Hurray! Hurray!"

His face lit up with a huge smile and then he died.

Wayne had seen something. It was something that made him happy, something bright. It gave him life.

Many people say that they see light just before they die. When I minister to the dying, I often tell them to go to the light, though I have no idea what it might look like.

Throughout the centuries, artists have painted Jesus and the saints with halos of light surrounding their faces. We try to depict some kind of lumination or radiance that comes when a person draws close to God.

Think about the fire we associate with Pentecost.

American culture has diluted and secularized Christmas and Easter. But no one can tame the Pentecost.

The early Christians believed that the day of Pentecost was equal in significance to Christmas and Easter. Pentecost is the day when the Holy Spirit descended and touched our lives. And when the Holy Spirit came down, there was lots of light.

The disciples had gathered together in an upper room. They felt lost and afraid, unsure of what to do now that Jesus had ascended into heaven. They knew they had been commanded to do Christ's work in the world, but they did not know how to begin. They needed a jump-start.

God came down in the form of fire, of inspiration and of light. The scripture describes *tongues of fire*. The whole room was bathed in light and this light illuminated everything, even the minds of the disciples. Suddenly, everything became clear. The disciples knew exactly what to do. They became inspired. (In fact, that is where the word "inspired" comes from, *in spiritus*.) They began to speak other languages. They felt a surge of divine power that had never happened before. God's potent presence visited. And it has not left us since.

No one can domesticate this holiday. It is too strange. You can't turn it into a fairy tale or use it as an excuse to shop. You can't make trinkets out of this story. The Pentecost rocks our world whenever we think of it. The Pentecost was so otherworldly, so absolutely mind-boggling. Either this event happened or it didn't, and, if it did, then the world as we know it changed that day. We became partners with God in the process of salvation.

From that day forward, our charge has been simple. We are asked to tell the story of Jesus, to burst out of our comfortable lives and tell everybody about the miracle of his existence and his love. We have a job to do.

Heaven touched earth on the day of the Pentecost, inviting us to live a resurrection life here and now. Don't wait for death. You can enter heaven even now. It can come to you right here. The light is all around you, just open your eyes.

Conclusion

Resurrection Moments

After years as a priest, I admit that there are some Sundays when I am tempted to stand in the pulpit, as Professor Evelyn Hutchinson suggested to me so many years ago, raise my arms to the sky, and simply shrug.

Resurrection cannot be explained with words. So I thank God for resurrection moments.

A few years ago, the Knight Foundation funded a project called Random Acts of Culture. On a random Saturday, they sponsored a miracle at Macy's in Philadelphia.

The place was packed with holiday shoppers and, (you can look this up on YouTube), the crowds seemed harried and impatient as they hurried through the store. Then something happened to happily disrupt this world of anxiety.

This particular Macy's store is a historic building with a grand pipe organ at its center. Suddenly the organ began to play. And then, people all over the store (who were actually professional musicians) began to sing Handel's Hallelujah Chorus.

"KING OF KINGS And LORD OF LORDS! KING OF KINGS and LORD OF LORDS! AND HE SHALL REIGN FOREVER AND EVER!"

All of a sudden the store changed. It became a vision of the Kingdom of Heaven. People began to sing along. They beamed. A baby was lifted into the air to dance. Old women and young children looked up radiantly. Some waved their arms exuberantly as if conducting the music. And oh, the smiles, the looks on the faces of these people. They were so beautiful.

I am convinced that Professor Hutchinson was right. When it comes to the resurrection, we will never fully understand the gift that has been given us. As human beings, we are forever standing before the mystery without answers, with our shoulders shrugging. But although we cannot comprehend resurrection, we can glimpse it. We can wake up and notice life beyond this life, a beauty that is somehow eternal, hidden in the midst of our harried lives.

I close with a resurrection moment, in the hopes that you will catch this glimpse of heaven itself with me and it will inspire you to glimpse resurrection in your own lives.

Max is my third son, my youngest child. His first day of kindergarten was bittersweet. He was so excited to join his brothers at school, to be in real school, to no longer be a baby. But I mourned. My youngest was beginning his journey to adulthood. I knew that I would never experience the first day of kindergarten with a child of mine again. And I always so loved being the mom of a preschooler.

In kindergarten, children still see see the world with fresh eyes. They are truly awake. My son will notice a large bug crawling across the sidewalk, even if we are rushing to a dental appointment. He sees shapes in the clouds and names them aloud. He is an ambassador to the kingdom of God, reminding me that it is right here, all around us. The resurrection life is right before his eyes.

As I saw him getting ready for kindergarten, I could not help thinking sad thoughts. Do I have to say good-bye to this child, as he is now, forever? Will I ever see him this way again?

I took a photo of him standing in the laundry room with his school uniform and his paper bag full of school supplies. He insisted on carrying that bag into the car and from the car to his classroom, even though it was half his size. He had written his name on the bag in those sloppy beautiful letters a five-year-old makes.

In the picture, Max has a grin on his face that defies explanation. Yes, he is excited, but he is also proud. It is the stance of a celebration, the face of one who is stepping into a new realm, of one who has completed a rite of passage and has emerged on the other side.

I look at that picture now and realize this was not the last time I would see such a smile on Max's face. There was something eternal in my love for him on that day. He reflected the face of God to me. And heaven will not be heaven without some part of him there, standing with his oversized bag and his face full of confidence and joy. He is part of the resurrection dimension for me now and will be forever.

When he came home from kindergarten, I asked him how his day went. He said:

"Mom, today there were rainbows coming out of my heart."

Resurrection can be seen even now. It can be touched by little children, by the truly hopeful, by anyone who opens their eyes to see.

www.ingramcontent.com/pod-product-compliance
Lightning Source LLC
Jackson TN
JSHW081317130125
77033JS00011B/324